JANE GOODALL

40 YEARS AT GOMBE

JANE GOODALL

40 YEARS AT GOMBE

A TRIBUTE TO FOUR DECADES OF WILDLIFE
RESEARCH, EDUCATION, AND CONSERVATION

*PRODUCED IN ASSOCIATION WITH
THE JANE GOODALL INSTITUTE*

STEWART, TABORI & CHANG
NEW YORK

Written by Jennifer Lindsey
Edited by Marisa Bulzone
Designed by Stephanie Whitehouse
Graphic production by Kim Tyner

Published in 1999 by
Stewart, Tabori & Chang
A division of U.S. Media Holdings, Inc.
115 West 18th Street
New York, NY 10011

Distributed in Canada by
General Publishing Company Ltd.
30 Lesmill Road
Don Mills, Ontario, Canada M3B 2T6

Library of Congress Catalog Card Number: 99–65401

The text of this book was composed in Meridien, Frutiger, and Lumpy.
Printed and bound in Hong Kong by Dai Nippon Printing Co., Ltd.

10 9 8 7 6 5 4 3 2 1
First Printing

"Only if we understand, can we care.

Only if we care, will we help.

Only if we help, shall all be saved."

-Jane Goodall

CONTENTS

An Unrivaled Woman

As we draw the curtain on twentieth-century primate behaviorists, one name stands out above all others: Jane Goodall. Her courage, tenacity, durability, and total commitment to one primate species, the chimpanzee, is simply unrivaled.

Initially, she possessed few pre-requisites to qualify for a scientific grant. While she had a modest demeanor, she was hardly the image one would project to become an "old African hand." When I first met Jane Goodall at National Geographic Society headquarters, she was obviously bright, but inexperienced, with a high-school equivalent education. Her "bush" experiences were honed into the genteel English countryside. I thought it very unlikely this attractive young woman would devote her life to studying chimpanzees at Gombe Stream, deep in the wild, remote forest of Tanzania. Fortunately, older and wiser men than I viewed Jane Goodall more favorably. Under the tutelage of Louis S. B. Leakey and with the support of Melville Bell Grosvenor, then President of the National Geographic Society, she was awarded a small grant from the Society's Committee for Research and Exploration in 1961, just as she was beginning her journey at Gombe.

Armed with binoculars and notepad, she set out to track these shy but little known primates. At first, just sighting a troop was rewarding. The chimps soon became accustomed to this fair-skinned bi-pedal creature who stalked them continuously. Eventually, they allowed her to sit in their presence—and a bond of acceptance and trust was created that prevails to this day.

Slowly the scientific community took notice of Jane's ability to mingle unobtrusively with chimpanzee troops, to identify and record behavior of individuals, and to build a compendium of continuous seasons of observations. Her reputation for serious scholarship reached Cambridge University, where she became the first person ever admitted to the doctoral program without a college degree. As we had now come to expect, she performed brilliantly to earn her Ph.D.

Her studies clearly reveal chimpanzees as tool makers, thus forcing scientists to redefine Homo sapiens. No longer was man the only "tool maker." From observation gleaned during forty years of fieldwork tracking four successive generations, she has verified that chimpanzees hunt, are carnivorous, vocalize to communicate, form complex family structures, and even exhibit the evils of genocide so often perceived to be limited to man. Through her scores of books, scientific articles, television programs, and lectures, the world has learned that chimpanzees are highly intelligent, endangered primates that must be preserved in the wild.

While her chimpanzee work is now legendary, Jane Goodall's trail-blazing path for other women primatologists is arguably her greatest legacy. During the last third of the twentieth century, Dian Fossey, Birute Galdikas, Cheryl Knott, Penny Patterson, and many more women have followed her. Indeed, women now dominate long-term primate behavioral studies worldwide.

Although I suspect she would really prefer to be at Gombe Stream, Jane travels constantly, persuading schoolchildren, scientists, opinion leaders, and heads of state of the dangers faced by wild chimpanzees. Few animal species—if any—are fortunate enough to have a worldwide champion as effective and indefatigable as Jane Goodall fighting to defend their well-being on Planet Earth.

Gilbert M. Grosvenor
Chairman, National Geographic Society

A Message from Jane Goodall

I am writing this in Gombe, on the veranda of my house overlooking Lake Tanganyika. The sun sinks, a huge red globe, behind the Congo hills in the west. What better place to reflect on the past, relive the memories of the day, dream of the future. This morning Fifi greeted me, as she has for the past few years, soon after my arrival in the forest. Somehow she always seems to know! She wandered toward me, her eighth and most recent infant clinging to her back, then sat and looked directly into my eyes. I gazed back. Fifi is the one chimpanzee who was alive when I first set foot on Gombe's shores in 1960 who is still alive today. There are some memories that are shared by us alone, memories of the early sixties, when Fifi herself was an infant. Presently she got up and carried her daughter away. I heard later, from Hilali Matama, who heads up our Tanzanian team of field staff, that they joined a big group with Fifi's oldest sons, Freud and alpha male Frodo.

I stayed on to absorb the forest's spirit. I thought about the early days when infant Fifi rode into camp on old Flo's back, the older Figan and Faben following. How enchanted Fifi had been when Flo gave birth again, to infant Flint. Fifi and I together had watched and learned from Flo the best qualities of motherhood—techniques that I had practiced when raising my own son, Grub, and that Fifi is still using as she raises her extraordinarily large family.

A fisherman's canoe glides past, silhouetted against the darkening water of the lake. In some ways Gombe has remained unchanged during the forty years since I first arrived with my mother, Vanne. The forest world of the chimpanzees has the same timeless quality that has nurtured my spirit during all the intervening years. Chimpanzees have been born and died, part of the endless cycle of nature. Students and field assistants from around the world have come and gone. And through it all we have followed the case histories of individuals and documented the history of the Gombe chimpanzee communities.

Results from our research and that from other studies in the field and in captivity have taught us much about these amazing beings. They differ from us genetically by only just over one percent. They hunt, share food, use and make tools. They form friendships that can endure throughout a life of up to sixty years. Their communication repertoire includes swaggering and punching, kissing and embracing. They show emotions like happiness, anger, sadness, and despair. They are capable of brutality—including primitive warfare—on the one hand; caring, compassion, and true altruism on the other.

Our understanding of chimpanzee behavior has given us a new perspective on our own position in the scheme of things, has blurred the line, once seen so sharp, between humans and the rest of the animal kingdom. We gain new respect not only for chimpanzees, but for the other amazing animal beings with whom we share the planet. And this urges a new sense of responsibility.

I was shocked to learn, during a conference in 1986, how rapidly chimpanzees were disappearing across their range in Africa. Numbering close to two million individuals at the turn of the century, a mere 150,000 (if that) remain, scattered (often in small fragmented groups that will almost certainly become extinct through inbreeding) across twenty-one African nations. Chimpanzees are threatened by habitat destruction as increasing numbers of people need ever more land. Gombe itself is a tiny 30 square miles of forest utterly surrounded by cultivated fields. Chimpanzees are caught in wire snares set by hunters for antelopes, pigs, and so on. The chimps can break the wire, but lose hand or foot from the agonizingly tightened loop or die of gangrene. There are dealers who pay hunters to shoot mothers and take their infants for the live animal trade.

But the greatest threat to the continued existence of chimpanzees in their last stronghold, the great Congo Basin, is the so-called "bush meat trade." Logging roads enable hunters from the towns to travel into the heart of the last remaining forests. Shooting everything, from chimps and gorillas to small antelopes and birds, they truck the meat to markets in the towns—where many people prefer the flesh of wild animals and will pay more. Subsistence hunting enabled humans to live in harmony with nature for hundreds of years. The new commercial hunting is a pathway to extinction—for the Great Apes and all other wildlife.

It is shocking, too, to learn the extent of the suffering inflicted on captive chimpanzees around the world. They languish in countless bad zoos, they are brutally treated in the entertainment industry. And the animal research industry has imprisoned hundreds in

5 foot by 5 foot prison cells where they must endure thirty years or more of solitary confinement without companionship, comfort, or love. Small wonder that many succumb to the crippling hopelessness of despair.

And small wonder that, knowing all this, I feel I must do all that I can to help. The Gombe chimpanzees have given me so much—how could I remain at peace with myself in my Gombe paradise knowing of the suffering of others, each with his or her own personality, each every bit as deserving of our concern as Fifi, Gremlin, and all the others. They all need our help—the wild chimpanzees and the captives sold or born into human servitude.

As I have been musing, here in Gombe, the sun has set, the sky is glowing dark red, and stars are beginning to twinkle out of the growing darkness. It seems so peaceful, yet "ethnic cleansing" is still taking place in neighboring Burundi to the north and refugees—women and children—still trickle into Tanzania each week. Across the lake, fierce fighting repeatedly erupts in the new Democratic Republic of the Congo, while in Congo-Brazzaville, repeated outbreaks of an ongoing civil war seriously affect our large sanctuary for orphan chimps. Yet because of dedicated staff, our projects continue.

Sitting here I'm feeling so grateful to so many people—all those who have helped over the years. This is a book compiled in their honor: For all the Tanzanians who welcomed Vanne and me when first we arrived, and those who have continued to support the research at Gombe ever since. For all the researchers, students, and field assistants who have contributed to the unique, long-term study at Gombe, especially Dr. Anthony Collins, without whom the field station might well have ended in the difficult days after the death of my late husband, Derek Bryceson. To those who made possible the founding of the Jane Goodall Institute to help me to achieve my goals, the late Ranieri di San Faustino and Genevieve "Genie" di San Faustino, our founder and president in America. And for all those to whom I have passed the baton to continue our JGI projects around the world—those who run our sanctuaries for orphan chimps in Africa, our

ChimpanZoo project, our reforestation and humanitarian efforts in Tanzania, and for all our amazing Roots & Shoots leaders and members who are working together for the future of Planet Earth. This book also celebrates the supporters, members, and friends of the Jane Goodall Institute, whose contributions enable our work to go on, with special gratitude to our major donors for their faith in the Institute, and in me, which has helped us in the past to survive some difficult times and helps us now as we move with confidence into the new millennium. This book honors also all the JGI staff who work in our administrative offices around the world, battling the mounds of paperwork, electronic mail, and millions of phone calls, ensuring that the work continues. And our board members and other volunteers who often put in so many hours and help so greatly.

Then some very special thanks: To Louis Leakey, without whom I would never have got to Gombe, to Hugo van Lawick, whose photos and films first introduced the Gombe chimpanzees to the world, to the National Geographic Society that supported the research for many years. And to the wonderful chimpanzee beings who have helped us better understand our own place in nature, the great Gombe characters such as Flo and Olly, Melissa and Gremlin, Goliath, Mike, Figan, and Goblin. Thanks and love to David Greybeard, my first chimpanzee friend who will always score highest in my affections. And to Fifi, with whom I share forty years of Gombe memories.

Lastly, thanks to my mother, Vanne Goodall, for the huge contributions she has made to my efforts. Not only did she encourage my childhood dream of going to Africa to live with animals, but her advice and wisdom over all the years have been of inestimable value.

Now, as we move into the next millennium, we look ahead to further years of conservation, education, and caring. We, the Jane Goodall Institute—all our staff, members, and friends—are determined to make a positive impact on our world. Won't you join us?

Jane Goodall

Chimpanzees can be recognized by their thick black coat and bare face. Chimpanzees' arms are longer than their legs and they possess opposable thumbs on their hands and big toes on their feet.

"If you really want something, and you work
hard enough, take advantage of opportunities,
and never give up, you will find a way."

-Vanne Goodall

The Beginning

ABOVE, LEFT: *Jane Goodall with Louis Leakey, Nairobi, Kenya, 1958.* CENTER: *At her original camp at Gombe Stream with David Greybeard.* RIGHT: *Writing field notes in her journal in the evening, 1961.* OPPOSITE: *Among the earliest and most significant of Jane's discoveries was that wild chimpanzees share with humans the ability to make and use tools—a skill previously thought to have set mankind apart from all other animals. She observed that the chimps would strip a twig of its leaves and then use the twig to probe a termite mound. Termites cling to the twig and are as easily eaten by the chimps as food from a fork.*

Yahaya Almasi bows his head; his weathered, brown face is wrinkled up in deep concentration. Talking in a soft voice he reflects on his first encounter with Jane Goodall, the strange young *Mzungu* woman who came in 1960 to the forest near his village of Babonogo, Tanzania, to study chimpanzees.

Yahaya had heard of the chimpanzees throughout his life. He'd heard of them coming into the village, to steal food or attack human babies. He'd heard of their humanlike behaviors, their great strength, and their mysterious communities in the deep recesses of the nearby forest. But what he remembers most was his grandmother's tale of their origin.

On the occasion of the Darkness Twice, his grandmother said, when the moon's shadow covers the sun in the heat of the day, everyone must hide inside their house, secure with food and firewood. If you are caught outside when the darkness descends, you will become a chimpanzee—just like those who live in the forest now. Listen carefully, she continued, when you hear the distant pounding of the tree buttress, the chimpanzees are dancing in the forest, singing "We used to be people, but now we are not."

17

Jane's mother, Vanne—a remarkable woman in her own right—recounts that her eldest daughter exhibited curiosity about the animal world from her earliest days. Jane grew up in England, and Vanne recalls returning home one afternoon during the war years to find the house curiously empty; everyone, she soon learned, was out searching for Jane, who at this point had been missing for several hours. By seven o'clock that evening, expressions were turning grave. "I don't remember who saw her first—a small, dishevelled figure coming a little wearily over the tussocky field by the hen houses," Vanne writes. "There were bits of straw in her hair and on her clothes but her eyes, dark ringed with fatigue, were shining. 'She's found,' someone called out and soon the searchers were all back and gathered around Jane in the stable yard. 'Wherever have you been?' 'With a hen.' 'But you've been away for nearly five hours. What can you possibly have been doing with a hen all that time?' 'Well you see I had to find out how hens lay eggs so I went into a hen coop to find out but as soon as I went in the hens went out so I went into an empty coop and sat in the corner and waited until a hen came in who didn't mind me there.' 'So then what happened?' 'A hen came at last.' Jane's eyes glowed with inner radiance. 'It was a long time but she came at last and then she laid an egg. I saw her. So now I know how a hen lays an egg.'...Dusk was fast gathering under the trees as we made our way back to the house. I had Jane firmly by the hand. She had just spent five hours crouched double in a stuffy hen coop but the result had made it all worthwhile. She had successfully and to her own entire satisfaction, completed her first animal research program. She had observed a hen lay an egg."

OPPOSITE LEFT: *Jane Goodall, circa 1935, with her beloved toy chimpanzee, Jubilee, a gift from her father. A real chimpanzee had been born at the London Zoo the year before, and named Jubilee in honor of the Silver Jubilee of the reign of King George V and Queen Mary. A limited number of very life-like toys were produced to commemorate the birth. A forecast of things to come, wherever Jane went, Jubilee went, too.* OPPOSITE RIGHT: *The intrepid Jane.* ABOVE: *Jane holding the beloved—and play-worn— Jubilee, with Nannie and Jane's sister, Judy.*

Many years later, when Yahaya heard of Jane Goodall's plans to study the chimpanzees, he thought she surely must be a brave woman—perhaps coming armed with voodoo—to want to live among these strange, wild animals of the rainforest.

The village elders were not alone in their belief that humans and chimpanzees shared a common origin. Louis Leakey, the famed paleontologist and anthropologist, believed wild chimpanzees could provide a glimpse into the lives of early humans. By studying the chimpanzees' behavior—their food gathering, their daily habits, and their social relations—we may have a better understanding of the evolution of Man.

The majority of chimpanzees live in the dense rainforests of Congo (formerly Zaire) and along the equatorial forest belt to the west coast of Africa. At that time, before the onslaught of commercial logging and human encroachment, most of this habitat was too remote and uninhabitable for human observers. Leakey chose the chimpanzee habitat of Gombe Stream Reserve, on the shore of Lake Tanganyika in the northwest corner of Tanzania, because it was easily accessible from the lakeshore. Then surrounded by more forest on three sides and the lake on the other, these 30 square miles of thick forest, rising up to open woodland and treeless ridges, Leakey believed, would be an ideal location for studying the behavior of our closest living relatives. His next step was to find someone to conduct the study. Fortunately for Leakey and for the chimpanzees he found Jane Goodall.

Jane was born in London, England, in 1934, the first daughter of Mortimer and Vanne Goodall. Throughout her childhood she showed a fascination for animals. When Jane was but a child, her nanny ran from Jane's room, telling Jane's mother Vanne that Jane had in her bed a handful of "horrible, pink, wriggling worms." "They're under her pillow," the nanny said, "and she won't let them go." Vanne remembers the day well.

"A peach-colored light from the setting sun was flooding the nursery. Jane's eyes were already closing, one hand was out of sight beneath the pillow. I pointed out that the

THE TIME LINE

JULY 16, 1960

JANE GOODALL BEGINS HER STUDY IN GOMBE STREAM GAME RESERVE, ACCOMPANIED BY HER MOTHER.

OCTOBER 1960

JANE OBSERVES A CHIMP USING A STRAW TO FISH OUT TERMITES, IT IS THE FIRST SCIENTIFIC DOCUMENTATION OF CHIMPANZEE TOOL USE.

NOVEMBER 1960

CHIMPANZEES ARE FIRST SEEN EATING MEAT.

MARCH 13, 1961

JANE RECEIVES A GRANT OF $1,400 FROM THE NATIONAL GEOGRAPHIC SOCIETY'S COMMITTEE FOR RESEARCH & EXPLORATION. IT IS THE FIRST OF TWENTY-SEVEN GRANTS THAT SHE WILL RECEIVE FROM NGS.

SUMMER 1961

DAVID GREYBEARD IS THE FIRST CHIMP TO EXPLORE THE GOMBE CAMP.

little creatures would find it altogether too hot and stuffy beneath the feathers. And after a tear or two she agreed to come with me to the dusky garden and return them to their rightful home....We did not realize then that the incident meant any more to Jane than the sorrow normally suffered by children when they lose a pet. But on looking back, I think it did. I believe her absorbing interest in the animal world was, even then, oddly objective....She was curious about them, and this insatiable curiosity about life, its origins and complexities, its mysteries and failures, has never left her."

From earthworms Jane turned her attention to hens, dogs, and other animals she met around her own garden. When she began to read, the stories of Dr. Doolittle and Tarzan unlocked her imagination. Before long, she dreamed of going to Africa.

Vanne's friends cautioned her about Jane's ambitions. "Tell Jane to dream about something she can achieve," they would say. "Don't give her false hope." But Vanne felt differently, and when Jane spoke of one day living in Africa to study animals, Vanne told her. "If you really want something, and you work hard enough, take advantage of opportunities, and never give up, you will find a way."

Jane's opportunity came when a school friend whose family had moved to Kenya invited her to visit. Jane saved up her fare working as a waitress and, once there, made an appointment to meet Dr. Louis Leakey, then Curator of the Coryndon Museum.

After one year of working under Leakey's direction in the museum, assisting with a paleontological dig in the now-famous Olduvai Gorge with Leakey and his wife Mary, and astounding Leakey with her unending knowledge of animals and their behavior, Leakey asked Jane to study the chimpanzees of Gombe Stream Reserve. She had no scientific training in animal study, indeed did not even hold an undergraduate degree. But, like Jane's mother Vanne, Leakey saw that she had an insatiable curiosity about the animal world, a strong determination to find the answers, and the necessary patience to await their discovery.

OPPOSITE: *Over the years, the chimpanzees at Gombe grew increasingly more comfortable with the human inhabitants of Gombe National Park. Here, Jane bends to take a closer look at infant Flint, being cradled by his sister Fifi.*

Yet there were a few obstacles to overcome before Leakey could send Jane out to begin her dream. She first needed the funds to support her preliminary investigation—funds for travel, food, and initial guides into the forest. With Leakey's help, she received a small grant from the Wilkie Foundation, in Des Plaines, Illinois, which supported studies of human and nonhuman primates. They then faced the concern of the British authorities, who refused to allow a young European woman to trek into the forests of the "Dark Continent" by herself. But Leakey prevailed. If they wouldn't let her travel alone, he reasoned, she could travel with the one person who always supported and encouraged her.

Nineteen months later, on July 16, 1960, Jane and her mother Vanne arrived at Kasekela, a campsite midway along the 10-mile shoreline of Gombe Stream Game Reserve. They were accompanied by Dominic, their African cook.

The early days were a struggle. Jane rose before dawn to search for the elusive chimpanzees. She trudged along the clear streams, hiked up the steep slopes, and crawled through the dense undergrowth to follow a far-off call. When she occasionally spotted a group of chimpanzees gathered in a tree, they ran away before she could get close enough to watch.

"When I am moving about through grass taller than my head, it is difficult to see anything. In order to continue my observations, I have to climb trees. Thus, as the rainy season progresses, my own habits become increasingly arboreal!" ABOVE: *Jane takes to the trees in pursuit of a suitable vantage point.* OPPOSITE: *A young chimp perches in a tree at Gombe.*

Slowly and cautiously, the chimpanzees accepted the presence of this strange white creature. And as she began to recognize and distinguish each unique face and character of her research subjects, she defied scientific protocol by giving them names, instead of numbers. Soon she was documenting the lives of Flo, her daughter Fifi, David Greybeard, Mr. Worzle, Mike, and Goliath.

With the Wilkie Foundation funding soon to run out, Jane was desperate to make a discovery significant enough to continue the funding. The discovery she made, in October 1960, not only continued her funding but changed the very way humans view

THE TIME LINE

1962
JANE ENTERS CAMBRIDGE UNIVERSITY AS A PH.D. CANDIDATE.

AUGUST 1963
JANE'S FIRST ARTICLE, "MY LIFE AMONG THE CHIMPANZEES," IS PUBLISHED IN **NATIONAL GEOGRAPHIC** MAGAZINE.

MARCH 28, 1964
JANE GOODALL MARRIES HUGO VAN LAWICK.

MARCH 1964
FLO GIVES BIRTH TO FLINT, WHOSE UPBRINGING PROVIDED A CHANCE TO OBSERVE CHIMPANZEE PARENTING FROM ITS BEGINNING.

SPRING 1964
MIKE GAINS DOMINANCE IN THE COMMUNITY, AND DEFEATS GOLIATH, BY CHARGING WITH NOISY KEROSENE CANS AND INTIMIDATING THE OTHER CHIMPS.

1963-1964
JANE RECEIVES THE FRANKLIN BURR AWARD FROM THE NATIONAL GEOGRAPHIC SOCIETY FOR HER CONTRIBUTION TO SCIENCE.

1964
THE GOMBE STREAM RESEARCH CENTRE IS FOUNDED.

the animal world. Jane witnessed David Greybeard stripping the leaves off a twig before poking it into a termite mound to retrieve the tasty insects. By doing this, David was modifying a natural object for a specific purpose—the first stages of tool making.

When the first grant money was completely gone, the National Geographic Society stepped in. On March 13, 1961, the NGS Committee for Research and Exploration issued Jane Goodall a grant of $1,400. It was the first of twenty-seven grants from the Society for a study that has gone on for forty years—the longest continuous field research ever conducted on a wild animal.

Although Vanne soon returned to England, her time at Gombe laid the groundwork for Jane's relationship with the local people. While Jane trekked into the forest following chimpanzees from dawn to dusk, Vanne stayed at the camp dispensing aspirin and other first-aid remedies to local villagers and fishermen.

One such fisherman was Yahaya Almasi. When he came into the small makeshift dispensary to receive medicine for malaria, he met the mother of the woman who studied the chimpanzees. He and his fellow fishermen discussed the stories of her discoveries as they fished each night on the lake, as Yahaya remembered his grandmother's tales of how chimpanzees came to be. And his curiosity grew.

In 1978, Yahaya left his life as a fisherman to join Jane Goodall and other Tanzanians in the groundbreaking research of Tanzania's chimpanzees. Although he no longer believes his grandmother's tale that chimpanzees were once people, he joins the rest of the world in marveling at the amazing similarities between humans and chimpanzees. And this, in the end, is the insightful gift Jane Goodall's determination has given to the world.

OPPOSITE: *In a family grouping that is very typical of chimpanzees, a mother, infant, and adolescent gather in a tree. Close relationships between mother and child—and often siblings— last a lifetime among chimpanzees.*

"Chimpanzees are more like us than any other living beings, not only in physiology, but also in social behavior, the emotions, and cognition. The line between humans and the rest of the animal kingdom, once thought to be so sharp, has become blurred. Chimpanzees bridge the gap between 'us' and 'them.'"

Fifi (far left) is a highly regarded female among the chimpanzees at Gombe. Here, she sits with a group of youngsters, while another adult chimp reclines.

"**From Nairobi** it took us more than five days to reach the Gombe Stream Game Reserve in Tanganyika, a 60-square-mile protected area set aside by the British where I would do my research. The Land-Rover was heavily overloaded, and most of the 840 miles of earth roads were in terrible condition," Jane Goodall reported of her first trip to Gombe. "Eventually, after innumerable delays, we reached Kigoma, a small European settlement overlooking Lake Tanganyika. There I hired the government launch to take us the last stage of the journey—the 16 miles up the lake to the Gombe chimpanzee reserve....As we traveled up the crystal-clear lake, I studied the terrain where I was to work. The mountains rise steeply from the narrow beach and are broken by innumerable valleys and gorges. The valleys are thickly forested, but the upper slopes become open woodland and many of the peaks and ridges are treeless."

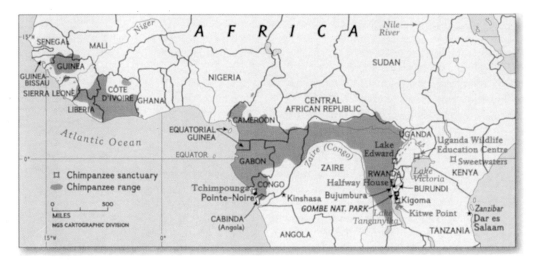

The Gombe Stream Game Reserve, now a 30-square-mile National Park, sits at the western edge of a tropical rain forest that cuts a narrow band across central Africa. Great Britain established the sanctuary after a 1942 safari confirmed the presence of apes in the area. It is believed that as recently as fifty years ago, the chimpanzee population in the wild may have been in the millions. Today, the population is less than 150,000. TOP: *The shoreline of Lake Tanganiyka at Gombe.* OPPOSITE: *Matriarch of the "F" family, Flo.*

The Chimpanzees

"How can she possibly be so ugly!" Those were the words of an early visitor to Gombe when seeing old Flo, one of Gombe's most beloved chimpanzees. Indeed, Flo was not a beautiful chimpanzee. She had ragged ears, a deformed nose, and teeth worn down to the gums. But she was one of the most popular female chimps in Gombe's Kasekela chimpanzee community, and people the world over admired her character, her mothering skills, and her diplomacy, as told by Jane in her books and articles.

Jane revealed to the world that each chimpanzee is an individual with his or her own unique personality, characteristics, and quirks. Indeed, since Jane's first *National Geographic* article landed in mailboxes in August 1963, we have followed the lives, loves, and hardships of the chimpanzees of Gombe as if they are members of a royal family. And their behaviors and life stories never fail to intrigue and inspire.

One of the first chimpanzees Jane came to know was David Greybeard. "David was less afraid of me from the start," she wrote in *In the Shadow of Man*. "I was always pleased when I picked out his handsome face and well-marked silvery beard in a chimpanzee group,

THE TIME LINE

SUMMER 1964
EVERED IS THE FIRST CHIMP SEEN USING CHEWED LEAVES AS A SPONGE TO SOAK UP WATER. THIS IS ANOTHER TOOL THAT IS FREQUENTLY USED BY THE CHIMPANZEES IN GOMBE.

SUMMER 1964
CHIMPANZEES ARE FIRST SEEN USING LEAVES TO CLEAN THEMSELVES AND WIPE WOUNDS.

1965
JANE GOODALL RECEIVES HER PH.D. IN ETHOLOGY, THE STUDY OF ANIMAL BEHAVIOR, FROM CAMBRIDGE UNIVERSITY. SHE IS THE EIGHTH AT THE UNIVERSITY TO BE AWARDED THE PH.D. WITHOUT FIRST RECEIVING HER BACHELOR'S DEGREE.

DECEMBER 1965
JANE'S SECOND ARTICLE "NEW DISCOVERIES AMONG AFRICA'S CHIMPANZEES," WITH PHOTOS BY HUGO VAN LAWICK, APPEARS IN **NATIONAL GEOGRAPHIC** MAGAZINE.

DECEMBER 1965
MISS GOODALL AND THE WILD CHIMPANZEES, AN HOUR-LONG PROGRAM PRODUCED BY THE NATIONAL GEOGRAPHIC SOCIETY, APPEARS ON U.S. NATIONAL TELEVISION.

for with David to calm the others, I had a better chance of approaching to observe them more closely."

David Greybeard was the first to come into her camp, to feast on the ripe fruit of the oil nut palm. When the palm tree stopped fruiting, Jane left bananas around the camp for David to eat should he wander through. He soon began to bring others with him—Goliath, and William, and sometimes a younger male—helping others to see that Jane was not a threat.

"One day, as I sat near him at the bank of a tiny trickle of crystal-clear water, I saw a ripe palm nut lying on the ground. I picked it up and held it out to him on my open palm. He turned his head away. When I moved my hand closer, he looked at it, and then at me, and then he took the fruit, and at the same time held my hand firmly and gently in his own. As I sat motionless he released my hand, looked down at the nut, and dropped it to the ground."

Because of David's comfort with Jane's presence, she owes thanks to him for her two first, and most significant, discoveries about the life of chimpanzees in the wild. Not only did David demonstrate to her that chimpanzees use and make tools, but it was David whom she saw eating the remains of a bushpig infant. Before this, chimpanzees were thought to be primarily vegetarians and fruit eaters.

"My own relationship with David was unique—and will never be repeated," Jane wrote in her 1986 book *The Chimpanzees of Gombe: Patterns of Behavior*. "When David disappeared during an epidemic of pneumonia in 1968, I mourned for him as I have no other chimpanzee before or since."

Another early visitor to Jane's camp was old Flo, perhaps unattractive to those who did not know her, but a wonderful chimpanzee in Jane's admiring eyes. When Jane first met Flo she had three offspring: Faben, Figan, and Fifi, the only daughter. At first Flo came to Jane's camp accompanied only by Fifi and adolescent Figan. But soon Faben began to join them, illustrating to Jane the ongoing relationship that can exist between grown chimpanzees and their mothers. When Flo became sexually attractive, she also began to bring her many male admirers into camp, as they followed her in hopes of mating. When the males discovered bananas in the camp, they, too, became regular visitors.

But it wasn't just Flo's introduction of other chimpanzees that distinguishes her as one of Jane's favorite Gombe personalities. As Jane describes her, "she was aggressive, tough as nails, and easily the most dominant of all the females at the time." She was a superb mother—easygoing, tolerant, playful and protective, but with enough discipline to keep Fifi in line and help her become a successful adult. Flo later gave birth to another son, whom Jane named Flint. Jane delighted in watching as Flo cared for her newborn infant with big sister Fifi desperate to have contact with her new brother.

The chimps were regular camp visitors at Gombe, initially attracted by the fruiting trees near the camp, and later by the bananas Jane offered when the fruits were no longer in season. ABOVE: *Fifi waits patiently for a banana, as Jane looks on.* RIGHT: *Jane grooms David Greybeard as he feasts on a banana.*

"Old Flo lay on her back in the early morning sunshine, her belly full of palm nuts, and suspended Flint above her, grasping one of his minute wrists with her large horny foot. As he dangled, gently waving his free arm and kicking with his legs, she reached up and tickled him in his groin and his neck until he opened his mouth in the play-face, or chimpanzee smile. Nearby Fifi sat staring at Flint, occasionally reaching out to touch her ten-week-old brother gently with one hand."

But Flo, inevitably, began to show her age. She was not strong enough to wean Flint when the time came, nor to care for her infant Flame, born nearly five years after Flint. Flame disappeared when Flo was too ill even to climb into a nest at night. Though she recovered somewhat after Flame's death, she still had little strength to care for Flint, who refused to establish his independence from his ailing mother. When Flo died in 1972, Flint fell into a state of depression. Lethargic and gaunt, he did not eat, or drink. Jane poignantly described Flint's last days in *Through a Window:* "The last journey he made, pausing to rest every few feet, was to the very place where Flo's body had lain. There he stayed for several hours, sometimes staring and staring into the water. He struggled on a little further, then curled up—and never moved again."

Flo's death left a void at Gombe, not only with the chimpanzees, but with Jane. And she is the only chimpanzee honored with an obituary in Britain's *Sunday Times*. Flo's legacy lives on in her daughter Fifi and her children. Fifi is the mother of seven: Freud, Frodo, Fanni, Flossi, Faustino, Ferdinand, and Flirt. (Another son, Fred, died in 1997.) By the mid-1980s Fifi had established herself as the top-ranking female. And, like Fifi's brother Figan, both Freud and Frodo have achieved the status of the community's alpha male. Fifi is the only one of the chimpanzees Jane met forty years ago who is still alive today. All other chimpanzees living in the Gombe's Kasekela community were born into a world that included Jane Goodall.

By observing Flo, Fifi and her offspring, the other community members, and the relationships among them, Jane learned that young chimpanzees stay with their mothers until they are at least seven years old, that adult chimpanzees form strong bonds, and, to her dismay, that rival communities can engage in brutal and bloody warfare.

Jane left Gombe temporarily in 1962 to pursue her doctorate in ethology (the study of animal behavior) from Cambridge University in England, becoming only the eighth

OPPOSITE: *Flo, matriarch of Gombe's "F" family, carries Flint on her back. Flo was mother to five Gombe chimps, all now deceased with the exception of Fifi, who is the mother of seven living chimpanzees.*

When Jane is at Gombe, she spends as much time as she possibly can with the chimpanzees. Ever the observer, she continues to carry a notebook in which she can record her field notes. OPPOSITE: *The majestic Mike was once the alpha male of the Kasekela group at Gombe. He was overthrown in 1971.*

person in the history of Cambridge University to be allowed to work for a doctorate without first having received a bachelor's degree. To avoid losing valuable data during her absence, she set up a program for visiting students to continue following and recording the behavior of the chimpanzees while she was away. And so began the Gombe Stream Research Centre. Since its inception in 1964, the Centre has become a launching pad for hundreds of students who longed to follow in Jane Goodall's footsteps, many of whom are now respected primatologists in their own right and trusted friends of Jane's.

But while visiting students and researchers stay for only months or years at a time, the Tanzanian field staff maintain a steady presence. Jane hired Rashidi Kikude in 1960, to carry her haversack and show her the terrain, and her first official field assistant, Hilali Matama in 1968, to assist the students and introduce them to the African bush. She described the arrangement in *The Chimpanzees of Gombe:* "Quite soon it became apparent that the field assistants could provide our research with an extremely important component: a core of individuals, with long-term commitment to the work, who were totally familiar with the chimpanzees, the terrain, and the food plants....they undoubtedly know more about following the chimpanzees through the forest, and perhaps understand more about their behavior, than most university-trained students."

Hilali Matama remains on staff today. He was joined by Eslom Mponog in 1971, Hamisi Mkono in 1972, and Yahaya Almasi in 1978. Other researchers have come and gone, but these four have remained committed to the job, to the research, to the forest, and to the chimpanzees.

Spending each day in the forest with the chimpanzees for up to thirty years, the Tanzanians have come to see the chimpanzees almost as family. When asked about his

THE TIME LINE

1966
FIFTEEN KASEKELA CHIMPS ARE AFFLICTED WITH POLIO. IN THE END, SIX DIE FROM THE DISEASE AND THE SURVIVORS HAVE AFFLICTIONS THAT LEAVE THEM DISABLED FOR THE REST OF THEIR LIVES.

1967
JANE GOODALL'S SON, HUGO ERIC LOUIS VAN LAWICK, NICKNAMED GRUB, IS BORN.

1968
HILALI MATAMA, JANE'S FIRST OFFICIAL FIELD ASSISTANT, IS HIRED AT THE GOMBE STREAM RESEARCH CENTRE.

1971
HUMPHREY DEFEATS MIKE AND TAKES OVER AS THE ALPHA MALE OF THE KASEKELA GROUP.

1971
JANE'S BOOK, **IN THE SHADOW OF MAN**, IS PUBLISHED. IT WOULD GO ON TO BE A BEST-SELLER.

1971
ESLOM MPONOG BECOMES THE SECOND FIELD ASSISTANT TO BE HIRED AT THE GOMBE STREAM RESEARCH CENTRE.

favorite chimpanzee over the years, Eslom's solemn face brightens, his eyes twinkle, and he sits forward with a ready smile. "Fifi has given birth to many good chimps," he says, "including Frodo, who is very strong and who is now alpha male. When I think of loving Frodo or Freud, it takes me back to Fifi."

Yahaya shares Eslom's love of the "F" family, but his allegiance is with Freud, former alpha male, and a gentler leader than his brother, Frodo, the current alpha male who delights in aggression. "Freud did not hit people or other chimps when he was the leader. He tried to associate well with others and he kept order in the community. When Freud did hit a chimp, Frodo was usually the choice—probably because he was trying to discipline his younger brother. Although Freud has lost his leadership to Frodo, I am pleased the leadership still lies within the family."

Eslom and Yahaya are not alone in their devotion to the Kasekela chimpanzees of Gombe Stream. Jane's books, documentaries, and speeches have brought the Gombe chimpanzees into the lives of people around the world, people who want to see that the research continues, that the chimpanzees are protected, and that Jane's goals are achieved. To this end, the Jane Goodall Institute for Wildlife Research, Education, and Conservation was founded in 1977 by Ranieri and Genevieve di San Faustino to help fund the continuing research and allow other supporters to contribute to its ongoing success. And just as Jane Goodall's goals and outlook have broadened throughout the years, so, too, has the mission of the Jane Goodall Institute.

OPPOSITE: *Frodo, a member of Gombe's well-known "F" family, is captured in a pose reminiscent of Rodin's* The Thinker.

Two of Gombe's most celebrated mothers—
Gremlin and Fifi—gather with some of their
children. From left to right are Ferdinand,
Gaia, Gremlin, Galahad, Fifi, and Faustino.

38

Gombe's F Family Family Tree

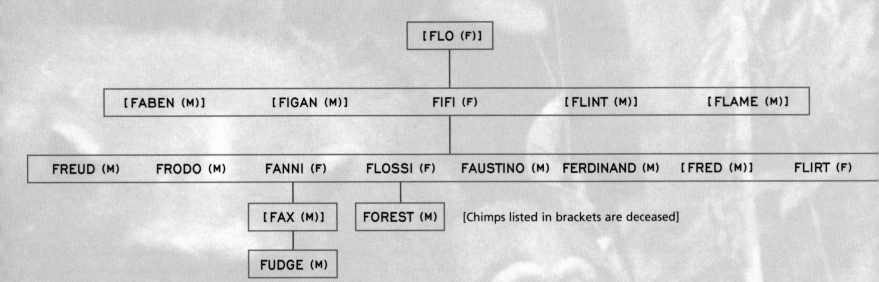

[FLO (F)]

[FABEN (M)]   [FIGAN (M)]   FIFI (F)   [FLINT (M)]   [FLAME (M)]

FREUD (M)   FRODO (M)   FANNI (F)   FLOSSI (F)   FAUSTINO (M)   FERDINAND (M)   [FRED (M)]   FLIRT (F)

[FAX (M)]   FOREST (M)   [Chimps listed in brackets are deceased]

FUDGE (M)

IN THE FORTY YEARS that Jane and her researchers have studied the chimpanzees at Gombe, the lives of these no-longer-mysterious animals has been likened to a soap opera. From the beginning, Jane has had the unique habit of naming her subjects. "People often ask me how I choose such names for individual chimpanzees," she has said. "My answer is that some names—such as Mrs. Maggs, Spray, and Mr. McGregor—simply come to mind. Strange as it may sound, some chimpanzees remind me of friends or acquaintances in some gesture or manner and are named accordingly." Such personalized names have helped to endear the chimpanzees of Gombe to the millions who have read of their adventures in the pages of *National Geographic*, or witnessed their behavior through the many televised documentaries on Jane's work. Most prominent of the four family genealogies that can be traced through Jane's research is the "F" family: Flo, a high-ranking female who died in 1972, and her offspring. Most successful of her five children were Figan, who became alpha male in 1973, and Fifi, who has seven living offspring of her own.

Flo

Figan

Flint

Fifi

Frodo

Freud

Fifi & Ferdinand

Fifi & Fred

Fanni & Fudge

Gremlin

Goblin, Gremlin &
Getty

Gremlin & twins
Gold & Glitta

FORTY YEARS OF RESEARCH among the chimpanzees at Gombe Stream represents the longest continuous study of any animal group ever conducted. Chimpanzees have a life expectancy in the wild of between forty and fifty years (and up to sixty in captivity), and each chimpanzee exhibits such individual characteristics that long-term study is necessary for a thorough understanding of their behavior. Chimpanzees are social animals with a fluid hierarchy in both males and females. These hierarchies are reinforced through communication using facial expressions, posture, touching and grooming, and vocalizations. Stable communities range in size from about twenty to one hundred individuals (there is an average of fifty at Gombe), but chimps often scatter into small temporary groups of three to six members.

Physically, the chimpanzee is our closest living relative in the animal kingdom; in fact, chimpanzees are biologically closer to humans than they are to monkeys, or even gorillas. The genetic differentiation between humans and chimpanzees is, remarkably, only just more than one percent. Moreover, the study of chimps at Gombe has resulted in fascinating behavioral similarities, the most significant being the discovery of chimpanzee tool making, meat eating, altruism, and—ten years into the study—observations of intercommunity violence.

Gombe National Park is a narrow strip of mountainous forest approximately 10 miles long and 3 to 5 miles wide. Dissected by thirteen steep-sided valleys carved by swift flowing streams, the park is home to approx-

imately 120 wild chimpanzees living in three distinct territorial communities. The Kasekela community, in the central part of the park, is the original study group and the main focus of forty years of chimpanzee research. Kasekela now whispers the memories of old Flo and her infant son Flint, gentle and accepting David Greybeard, high-ranking Melissa, tragic Olly, and Passion, who, with her daughter Pom, perpetrated infanticide. To the north of Kasekela is the Mitumba chimpanzee community, on which continuous research began within the past ten years. And to the south are the Nyasanga chimps, about which very little is still known.

In 1970, the Kasekela group suddenly began to divide. Seven males and three females with offspring broke away and established

Goblin

David Greybeard

themselves in the southern part of their home range. By the end of 1972, this group was recognized as the Kahama community. During the next four years, the Kasekela males systematically hunted down and brutally attacked the members of the smaller Kahama community, until nearly all but the adolescent females had been killed or had disappeared.

Kasekela remains the main study group at Gombe National Park, now home to Flo's top-ranking daughter Fifi and her children, including alpha male Frodo and former alpha Freud; Melissa's offspring Goblin and Gremlin, with Gremlin's children Galahad, Gaia, and twins Gold and Glitta; along with many others. Full-time habituators now follow and research the Mitumba community in the north, which gained fame in 1995

when Rafiki gave birth to twins, Roots and Shoots. In 1996, a severe respiratory illness claimed the lives of Rafiki, Roots, Shoots, and five other community members, including the alpha male Cusano—a devastating loss to the community of only twenty-nine chimpanzees. In the summer of 1999, researchers again began trekking into the southern area of the park to search for and study the elusive southern community of chimpanzees.

The Gombe Stream Research Centre is now run by Dr. Anthony Collins, who heads up the research of the park's olive baboons, and Dr. Shadrack Kamenya, who is in charge of chimp research. Bill Wallauer is a full-time videographer in the park, documenting the chimpanzees' behavior for archives, education, and research.

Behavior

The structure of the chimpanzee brain is startlingly similar to that of the human. Many aspects of their behavior and social relations, emotional expression, and needs, are also similar to those of humans. Various mental traits once regarded as unique to humans have been convincingly demonstrated in chimpanzees: reasoned thought, abstraction, generalization, symbolic representation, and concept of self. Non-verbal communication includes hugs, kisses, pats on the back, play tickling, swaggering, punching, and so on. Many of their emotions, such as joy and sadness, fear and despair, are similar to or the same as our own.

The chimpanzee life cycle is not very different from that of humans. Infancy lasts for a five-year period, followed by childhood, and then adolescence, which lasts from about nine to thirteen years. The onset of old age occurs at about forty years.

There are, in particular, close parallels between the chimpanzee infant and the human child. Both have the capacity for endless romping and play, are highly curious, learn by observation and imitation, and above all, need constant reassurance and attention. For both, affectionate physical contact is essential for healthy development.

Although chimpanzees most often live in primary, uncut forest, they are also found in secondary re-growth forests, open woodlands, bamboo forests, and swamp forests. Despite their adaptability, the intrusion of logging operations into their natural habitat have been found harmful to chimpanzee populations.

Nomadic, chimpanzees spend their days roaming within a specific territory, although how far they travel in a day depends on the abundance of food. Each chimpanzee builds a new nest for itself each night, although infants will sleep with their mothers until the age of five, or until the next infant is born. During the rainy season, chimps will also build nests high in the trees during the day, so that they will not have to nap on the cold, damp ground. In the dry season, they prefer to sleep in the shade of trees. Interestingly, they make no serious attempt to shelter themselves from the rain.

In her *National Geographic* article "My Life Among the Wild Chimpanzees," Jane reported: "The construction of a nest, I found, is simple and takes only a couple of minutes. After choosing a suitable foundation, such as a horizontal fork with several branches growing out, the chimpanzee stands on

Young chimps play much of the day, gaining valuable social skills and strength for life as adults.

this and bends down a number of branches from each side so that the leafy ends rest across the foundation. He [or she] holds them in place with his feet. Finally he bends in all the little leafy twigs that project around the nest, and the bed is ready. But the chimpanzee likes his comfort, and often, after lying down for a moment, he sits up and reaches out for a handful of leafy twigs which he pops under his head or some other part of his body. Then he settles down again with obvious satisfaction."

Chimpanzees are mainly vegetarians and eat fruit, leaves, seeds, and flowers. But they will also feast on ants, honey, eggs, and caterpillars. Occasionally they hunt, kill, and eat small and medium size mammals, especially young bush pigs, monkeys, or antelope. If a younger chimp has made the kill, the carcass is often shared among a small group. But if the prey is in the possession of a high-ranking male, other chimpanzees will gather round and beg for shares.

Chimpanzees stay with their mothers until they are seven or eight years of age, and subsequently return, from time to time, throughout life.

47

Tool Making

Before Jane Goodall began her research, it was thought that the ability to craft and use tools was specific to Homo sapiens. We now know that chimpanzees use tools to solve a great range of problems. Primary among these at Gombe is the "fishing" of termites from underground nests with the aid of a stem of grass or a twig. Jane describes this most important of her discoveries as follows: "Termites are a major part of the chimpanzee diet for a two-month period. The termite season starts at the beginning of the rains, when the fertile insects grow wings and are ready to leave the nest. At this time, the passages are extended to the surface of the termite heap and then sealed lightly over while the insects await good flying weather. Chimpanzees are not alone in their taste for termites—baboons in particular have a fondness for the juicy insects, but must wait until they fly and then take their turn, together with the birds, at grabbing the termites as they leave the nest.

"The chimpanzees forestall them all. They come along, peer at the surface of the termite heap and, where they spy one of the sealed-off entrances, scrape away the thin layer of soil. Then they pick a straw or dried stem of grass and poke this carefully down the hole. The termites, like miniature bulldogs, bite the straw and hang on grimly as it is gently withdrawn.

"As the straw becomes bent at the end, the chimpanzee breaks off the bent pieces until the tool is too short for further use. Then it is discarded and a new one picked. Sometimes a leafy twig is selected, and before this can be used the chimpanzee has to strip off the leaves.

"In doing so—in modifying a natural object to make it suitable for a specific purpose—the chimpanzee has reached the first crude beginnings of tool making."

Chimpanzees will often not wait to find a termite hill to create their "fishing" tool, but carry it with them at the ready. This particular tool use is a learned behavior—passed on from one generation to the next through observation and imitation. Chimpanzees at Gombe use other tools, such as sticks to enlarge holes in trees to search for honey and tree ants, and to investigate termite holes.

"I have watched chimpanzees fish this way for two hours at a time, picking dainty morsels from the straw and munching them with delight. When they don't have much luck with one hole, they open another and try again."

ABOVE LEFT: *A mother and child strip leaves from a twig to make a tool for "fishing" termites. This behavior is passed on from mother to child.* OPPOSITE: *Goblin uses a stripped twig to poke down into a termite hole, where the termites will cling fast to the branch.*

Leaves are another tool utilized by chimpanzees for a number of different purposes. They are used to make sponges, which they use to sop up moisture in the hollow of a tree trunk when the water level gets too low for liquid to be sucked up with the lips. Chewed leaves are dipped into the water and then the leaves are sucked on. Leaves are also used to brush away bees and driver ants, and as napkins, to wipe away dripping fruit juice.

Chimpanzees will use sticks and rocks to smash fruits that are too hard to bite open, and, in some parts of Africa, chimps use sticks as levers. Tools are not only used to obtain food and water. Adult males will hurl sticks, branches, and rocks, against other chimpanzees, baboons, and humans.

ABOVE: *Jane catches up on the latest news with members of the permanent research staff at Gombe.*

OPPOSITE: *A branch filled with termites makes a tasty snack, a favorite of the chimpanzees.*

ABOVE: *Chimpanzees have a sophisticated repertoire of sounds and gestures to communicate with each other.* OPPOSITE: *Nonverbal communication, including grooming, is also an important aspect of the chimpanzees' social structure.*

Family Groups

Close, supportive, and affectionate bonds develop between family members and other individuals within a chimpanzee community, which can persist throughout their lives. Chimpanzees cooperate within their community in grooming, hunting and defense, but aggression can occur between two communities that may result in injury and death for some members.

Chimpanzees become sexually mature when they are between eight and thirteen years old. Female chimps are promiscuous within their group, often mating with several males. Females usually have babies every five years, but a mother is unlikely to raise more than three offspring to full maturity during her lifetime because of the high infant mortality rate. The gestation period is approximately eight months.

When a chimpanzee is born, it is practically helpless. It is, in fact, quite similar to a human baby, except that a chimpanzee is born with great strength in its hands and feet. This enables it to cling to its mother, holding onto her hair as she moves about. Chimpanzee babies will begin to take one or two steps at roughly four months, albeit cautiously. Chimps usually are weaned at five years, but stay with their mothers until they are at least seven.

"There is a great deal in chimpanzee relationships to remind us of our own behavior. More, perhaps, than many of us would care to admit."

Young female chimps will shape their mothering skills by watching others and by grooming, carrying, and playing with younger siblings or the infants of others when allowed. The father plays no role in child-rearing, but patrols the boundaries of the territory, protecting its resources for the females and young.

Young chimps are very active, and among Jane's earliest observations was the group's good-natured tolerance of youngsters at play. "I once watched little Fifi tormenting an adolescent male, Figan. He was resting peacefully when Fifi hurled herself onto him, pulling his hair, pushing her fingers into his face, biting his ears," she writes. "She swung above him, kicking out, while he indulgently pushed her to and fro with one hand. Finally, exhausted for the moment, she flung herself down beside him."

Most chimps remain in their natal group throughout their lifetime, but adolescent females may also join other communities. Older siblings, including males, have been known to adopt young brothers or sisters if the mother dies. For the male chimp, puberty begins at eight years of age and, as is the

case for humans, adolescence can be stressful. The young male's status within his family group will begin to improve as he grows older and his mother will have to treat him with deference. But while children are generally indulged and tolerated, the adolescent male must learn to show respect to the older males, lest he be attacked. In this time of uncertainty, adolescent males often lose confidence and may spend greater amounts of time alone or with their mothers.

A fascinating aspect of family relationships that Jane and her researchers have observed at Gombe is that between mothers and their infant children. After forty years of collecting data, it is clear that the mothering skills of female chimpanzees can differ greatly. Flo and Passion provide an interesting contrast: both mothers were high-ranking females, but had different relationships within the community. Flo was very sociable and had relaxed relations with adult males. She was an attentive and tolerant mother. Passion, however, was asocial. She was callous and indifferent to her daughter Pom and her relations with community males were tense. Passion's behavior turned violent. She killed an infant chimp and shared the meat with her offspring. Apparently exhibiting learned behavior, Pom later helped her mother kill two more infants.

Certainly the most poignant of these mother-child pairs is Flo and her son Flint. So closely tied to Flo that he never achieved independence, Flint died at age eight and a half, after spending three weeks grieving for his mother.

Within each chimpanzee community, there are high-ranking females and low-ranking males as well as a single, alpha male. Observations at Gombe have shown that—unlike other species—there appears to be no certain advantage to the position of alpha male among chimpanzees, other than

ABOVE: *Access to food is, in part, determined by a chimpanzee's rank within its community.*
OPPOSITE: *Cusano and Rafiki mating. Female chimps are not monogamous and will mate freely within the group.*

THE TIME LINE

1975
JANE MARRIES HER SECOND HUSBAND, THE HON. DEREK BRYCESON, MEMBER OF TANZANIAN PARLIAMENT.

1977
THE JANE GOODALL INSTITUTE FOR WILDLIFE RESEARCH, EDUCATION AND CONSERVATION IS ESTABLISHED, IN SAN FRANCISCO.

OCTOBER 21, 1977
MELISSA GIVES BIRTH TO TWINS GYRE AND GIMBLE. ONLY GIMBLE SURVIVES.

MAY 1979
JANE REPORTS ON NEW DISCOVERIES IN HER ARTICLE "LIFE AND DEATH AT GOMBE," FOR **NATIONAL GEOGRAPHIC** MAGAZINE.

1980
JANE RECEIVES THE ORDER OF THE GOLDEN ARK, THE WORLD WILDLIFE AWARD FOR CONSERVATION, PRESENTED BY PRINCE BERNHARD OF THE NETHERLANDS.

achieving a status that commands respect. Alpha male status does not guarantee exclusive mating rights, nor does it gain him any great advantage over another when it comes to gaining access to food. Such status will, however, protect him from the attacks of other males, except, of course, in the instance of a challenge.

Females of high rank receive preference, most importantly in terms of access to food sources. This, in turn, can increase the survival rate among their offspring. In addition, the offspring of a high-ranking female will usually benefit from its mother's position in the community, and move toward adulthood with more confidence and a better ability to navigate the group's social structure.

Chimpanzees at Gombe mate and give birth throughout the year, although it appears that they will mate more aggressively and frequently during September and October, which is spring in Tanzania.

ABOVE: *Rafiki and her twins, Roots and Shoots. Born in 1995, they were only the second set of twins observed at Gombe. Sadly, all three were lost in 1997, victims of a respiratory illness that swept through their group, claiming eight lives within the northern community.*
OPPOSITE: *Flint, depressed and lethargic, mourns the death of his mother Flo.*

ABOVE: *Here, male chimpanzees of the Mitumba community curry favor with the alpha male, through grooming.* OPPOSITE: *Grooming eases social tensions, establishes and reinforces friend-ships, and strengthens familial bonds.*

Social Behavior

Relationships among adult chimpanzees are more complex than had been thought before Jane Goodall came to Gombe. Prior to her studies, chimps were thought to live in harems, with a single alpha male and several females.

Among her earliest observations was the variety of ways that chimpanzees will express their feelings. Chimpanzees are highly extroverted and when two groups meet, there is often a great show on the part of the males, consisting of loud calls, drumming on tree trunks, and shaking of branches. The females and young chimps will scream and run out of the way. Controversy within the group is usually settled by furious gestures and loud noise, rather than physical attack.

The "language" of chimpanzees is highly developed. They have a variety of sounds, each of which expresses a specific emotion and is understood by other chimps. Jane has described these sounds as ranging "from the rather low-pitched 'hoo' of greeting, and the series of low grunts that is heard when a chimpanzee begins to feed on some desirable food, to the loud, excited calls and screams which occur when two groups meet. One call, given in defiance of a possible predator, or when a chimpanzee, for some reason, is angry at the approach of another, can be described as a loud 'wraaaah.' This is a single syllable, several times repeated, and is one of the most savage and spine-chilling sounds of the African forest. Another characteristic call is a series of hoots, the breath drawn in audibly after each hoot, and ending with three or four roars. This is the cry of a male chimpanzee as he crosses a ridge. It seems to be an announcement to any other chimpanzees who may be in the valley below: 'Here I come.'"

"Chimpanzees are so inventive. They do lots of things they don't need to for survival."

Chimpanzees also communicate by touch and gesture. A mother will touch her child when she is about to move away, and may tap on a tree trunk when she wants the youngster to come down. A chimpanzee who wants food will hold out a hand—palm up—in a very human-like gesture of begging. Chimps exchange gestures of greeting and friendship as well as calls, and two friends greeting each other after a separation may embrace, kiss, or pat one another on the back.

ABOVE: *Although they do express themselves with a wide range of vocalizations, chimpanzees also communicate through touch. This group of chimpanzees is arranged in a conga line of grooming.*
OPPOSITE: *Chimpanzees can spend up to two hours grooming each other.*

THE TIME LINE

Although chimpanzees will go to bed earlier and rise later during the rainy season, they are also more physically active during this time. Often, at the start of a heavy rain, a male will break into a run, slapping the ground or hitting out at a low branch as he passes. This behavior, when large groups are present, may develop into a fascinating display that Jane has dubbed their "rain dance." Jane describes the first time she encountered this spectacular display in her book, *In the Shadow of Man*.

"At about noon the first heavy drops of rain began to fall. The chimpanzees climbed out of the tree and one after the other plodded up the steep grassy slope toward the open ridge at the top. There were seven adult males in the group, including Goliath and David Greybeard, several females, and a few youngsters. As they reached the ridge the chimpanzees paused. At that moment the storm broke. The rain was torrential, and the sudden clap of thunder, right overhead, made me jump. As if this were a signal, one of the big males stood upright and as he swayed and swaggered rhythmically from foot to foot I could just hear the rising crescendo of his pant-hoots above the beating of the rain. Then he charged off, flat-out down the slope toward the trees he had just left. He ran some thirty yards, and then, swinging round the trunk of a small tree to break his headlong rush, leaped into the low branches and sat motionless.

"Almost at once two other males charged after him. One broke off a low branch from a tree as he ran and brandished it in the air before hurling it ahead of him. The other, as he reached the end of his run, stood upright and rhythmically swayed the branches of a tree back and forth before seizing a huge branch and dragging it farther down the slope. A fourth male, as he, too, charged, leaped into a tree and almost, without breaking his speed, tore off a large branch, leaped with it to the ground, and continued down the slope. As the last two males called and charged down, so the one who had started the whole performance climbed from his tree and began plodding up the slope again. The others, who had also climbed into trees near the bottom of the slope, followed suit. When they reached the ridge, they started charging down all over again, one after the other, with equal vigor.

"The females and youngsters had climbed into trees near the top of the rise as soon as the displays had begun, and there they remained watching throughout the whole performance....I could only watch, and marvel at the magnificence of those splendid creatures. With a display of strength and vigor such as this, primitive man himself might have challenged the elements."

Chimpanzees are built for climbing trees: their long arms, keen eyesight, and opposable thumbs on both hands and feet help them navigate the high treetops in search of fruit, on a hunt, or when building their nests to bed down for the night.

"When I first started at Gombe, I thought the chimps were nicer than we are. But time has revealed that they are not. They can be just as awful."

Pom, shown above, and her mother Passion were seen to kill and eat three Kasekela infants and were suspected to have killed a total of ten newborns during a four-year period. The killings came to an end in 1977.

Aggressive Behavior

Threatening gestures and calls are more frequent in chimpanzees than are actual physical fights. When fights do break out, the most common causes are competition for status, defense of family members, and frustration that leads an individual who has been thwarted by one stronger to turn and vent his aggression on a smaller or weaker bystander. Fights may break out between individuals competing for food or between males competing for the same female. Males may attack females seemingly in order to drum into their victims, again and again, that theirs is a male-dominated society.

A chimpanzee community has a home range within which its members roam in nomadic fashion. At Gombe, the home range of the main study community has fluctuated between 5 and 8 square miles. The adult males, usually in groups of three or more, quite regularly patrol the boundaries, keeping close together, silent, and alert. If the patrol meets up with a similar-sized group from another community, both sides, after exchanging threats, are likely to withdraw discreetly back into home ground. But if a single individual is encountered, or a mother and child, then the patrolling males usually chase and, if they can, attack the stranger.

In 1970, the main study community at Gombe began to divide. Seven males and three females with offspring established themselves in the southern (Kahama) part of the original home range. During the next two years these individuals returned to the north less and less frequently. By 1972, they had become a completely separate community.

For a time the situation seemed fairly peaceful. If groups of the northern (Kasakela) and southern communities met near their common boundary, the males would display, calling loudly, drumming on the trees, dragging branches as they charged back and forth. These displays served to persuade members of the neighboring groups to turn back into their respective home ranges.

Then, in early 1974, violence broke out among the two groups when five chimpanzees from the Kasekela community caught a single male of the Kahama group. By the end of 1977, it was certain that only one of the southern males still survived. The researchers at Gombe had observed a phenomenon rarely recorded in field studies: the gradual extermination of one group of animals by another, stronger group.

ABOVE, LEFT AND RIGHT: *Male chimpanzees spend thier days in mixed groups, feeding, resting, and patrolling territorial borders, as shown above. Sometimes they climb a tall tree and stare out at the "hostile" territory of an adjacent community.* LEFT: *Although primarily vegetarian, chimpanzees sometimes hunt and kill for food. In this case, the chimpanzees had found and stolen a bushbuck that was killed by baboons. Fifi dominated the adult males in her group to keep the prize. She did not share until completely satisfied.*

CHIMPANZEE FACTS

During forty years studying free-ranging chimpanzees at the Gombe National Park, Jane Goodall, her students, and field staff have observed all aspects of behavior, the life cycle from birth to death.

GENERAL

- Chimpanzees show intellectual abilities once thought unique to humans.
- They share, with us, emotions such as joy and sadness, fear and despair.
- They catch or can be infected with all human contagious diseases (except cholera).
- The structure of their DNA differs from ours by just more than one percent.
- Humans and chimps can exchange blood of the same type.
- But chimps do not swim, cry tears, or bury their dead.

FEEDING

- Omnivorous, like humans, chimpanzees eat meat, eggs, and insects, as well as fruits, leaves, shoots, blossoms, stems, and bark.
- They will eat mouthfuls of leaves with each bite of meat, as we eat vegetables.
- They are successful hunters, sometimes showing sophisticated cooperation.
- Cannibalism among them has been documented.

TOOLS

- Chimpanzees use many objects as tools, and also modify them if necessary, such as grass stems, or twigs stripped of leaves, to extract termites from their nests.
- They use leaves to wipe dirt off themselves or, crumpled as sponges, to sop up water they cannot reach with their lips.
- They use rocks and branches as weapons during aggressions.

SHARING

- Most sharing among chimpanzeees occurs between mothers and infants. But adults will share meat after a successful kill, in response to begging.
- One adolescent female, on three occasions, climbed down from a tall tree with food in her mouth and hand, to feed her old sick mother.

COMMUNICATION

- Chimpanzees have a rich repertoire of calls, each in their own distinct voice.
- Many of their postures and gestures are uncannily like some of our own: When greeting, chimpanzees embrace, hold hands, kiss, and back pat. This helps calm excited or nervous individuals.
- Aggression among chimpanzees includes waving arms, swaggering, punching and kicking. Females sometimes scratch and pull each other's hair.
- Disputes between chimpanzees are often solved by making threats.
- Attacked victims adopt a submissive appeasing posture usually triggering a reassurance gesture—patting, embracing, or kissing—from the aggressor, restoring social harmony.
- Long sessions of social grooming serve to reinforce friendships and provide relaxation.

SOCIETY

- Chimps live in a complex society. All fifty or so members of the community know each other as individuals.
- Their's is a male-dominated society where adult males compete for top rank (alpha male) and may reign for as long as ten years.
- Chimpanzees are aggressively territorial.
- Males patrol boundaries regularly.
- During a four-year period, males of a larger community systematically hunted and killed individuals of a smaller neighboring community.

LIFE STAGES

- A chimpanzees's first tooth appears at about three months. Permanent teeth start coming in during the fifth year.
- A chimpanzee takes its first tottering steps at five months and walks unsteadily for the first two years or more.
- Solid food is not an important part of the chimpanzee diet until the age of three.
- Chimpanzees experience a long period of infant dependence on the mother. An infant suckles, rides the mother's back, and sleeps in the night nest during the first five years.
- Male puberty is reached around nine and maturity around thirteen. Adolescence is a frustrating time and he becomes more aggressive, although he is extra-cautious with adult males who fascinate him, yet frighten him.
- The female develops her first small swellings of the sex skin when she is about eight and is mated by juvenile males, but he is not able to conceive until eleven or twelve.
- Wild chimpanzees begin to look old when they are about forty years old. Captive chimps have lived as long as sixty-five years.

REPRODUCTION

- Females generally give birth to one infant at a time. Only three sets of twins are known to have been born in Gombe since Jane's research began.
- There is an interval of five years between live births. If an infant dies, the mother becomes pregnant again within a couple of months.
- Pregnancy is eight lunar months.
- A sexually receptive female is mated by males one after the other.
- Infant mortality is high, and a female is unlikely to raise more than three offspring to full social maturity during her lifetime.
- Excessive inbreeding is avoided through a sexual inhibition—like an incest taboo—that typically prevents mating between mother and son and, to some extent, between brother and sister.
- Some females have more sex appeal than others. Often an old and experienced female is more popular than a young and nervous female.

THE FAMILY

- It is the mother who is responsible for raising her infants. There are good chimpanzee mothers and bad ones. Most, however, are extraordinarily patient, tolerant, affectionate, and playful.
- There is no special father/child relationship.
- An older sibling will play with, groom, and help to protect the new baby.
- Bonds between family members are close, affectionate, supportive, and may last through life.
- After the death of a mother, her infant—even though nutritionally independent—may be unable to recover from the trauma and may die.
- Older siblings, males too, may typically adopt young brothers or sisters if the mother dies.
- An adult sterile female has adopted no fewer than three orphaned infants during a two-year period.

A young chimp sits contemplatively in the elbow of a tree limb at Gombe. Chimps travel on the ground, but spend much time in the trees—feeding and sleeping.

"The least I can do is speak out for the hundreds of chimpanzees who, right now, sit hunched, miserable and without hope, staring out with dead eyes from their metal prisons. They cannot speak for themselves."

The Realization

ABOVE*: Oscar was born in captivity, the son of a chimpanzee living in the Sweetwaters Sanctuary near Nanyuki, Kenya. His mother was captured by poachers in the wild. Once confiscated from the poachers, she was brought to the sanctuary to live among other chimpanzees. Although the Institute does not condone breeding within the sanctuaries, sometimes the birth control methods do fail. Oscar is an active, healthy young chimpanzee who brings great joy to the many adult chimps in the sanctuary whose own childhoods were cut tragically short.* OPPOSITE*: Today, Gombe National Park is a refuge for Jane, who spends most of her days traveling and speaking on environmental issues to a world-wide audience.*

In 1968, the Tanzanian government declared Gombe Stream Reserve a National Park, forbidding all hunting, cutting down of trees, or otherwise destroying the forest's biodiversity—a firm acknowledgment of the importance of protecting this tiny 30-mile stretch of forest, only 5 miles wide at its greatest expanse. But this protected area is but a tiny forest "island" in the middle of Africa. Chimpanzees—150,000 of them—also live outside of Gombe's forest paradise, along the equatorial forest belt across Africa, in the vast rain forests of Congo (formerly Zaire), in Burundi, Uganda, and up into West Africa.

For many of these chimpanzees, there is no such protection. The continent's ever-growing human population is slowly but steadily encroaching on the virgin forest land—chopping trees for firewood; clearing undergrowth for subsistence farmland; hunting the forest animals to sell their meat at markets; and taking living infant chimpanzees from their dead mothers' arms to sell as pets.

When Jane realized chimpanzees across Africa were endangered, she made a decision that would change forever the face of the conservation movement. Using the fame and

OCTOBER 1986
MELISSA, MOTHER OF GOBLIN, GREMLIN, AND GIMBLE, DIES.

1986
THE CHIMPANZEES OF GOMBE: PATTERNS OF BEHAVIOR, JANE'S FOURTH BOOK, IS PUBLISHED.

MARCH 1987
AN OUTBREAK OF PNEUMONIA AFFLICTS THE CHIMPANZEES, KILLING ELEVEN. IT IS THE WORST EPIDEMIC SINCE THE POLIO OUTBREAK IN 1966.

1987
JANE RECEVES THE ALBERT SCHWEITZER AWARD FROM THE ANIMAL WELFARE INSTITUTE IN WASHINGTON, DC.

1987
AFTER THREE-YEAR-OLD MEL'S MOTHER DIED OF PNEUMONIA, HE WAS "ADOPTED" BY AN ADOLESCENT MALE, SPINDLE—THE FIRST TIME THAT A NONRELATED CHIMP IS OBSERVED TO ADOPT AN ORPHANED YOUNGSTER.

recognition she had gained from her *National Geographic* articles and documentaries, Jane Goodall left the solitude and beauty of the Gombe forest and the chimpanzees whom she loved almost like family, to travel the world, raising awareness of the plight of our closest living relatives—and raising money to fight to save them.

Her home in Gombe became not a base but a get-away, a place to replenish her energy and gain inspiration to continue her campaign to save the chimpanzees. Though she still monitors and directs the research, she began to relinquish the day-to-day responsibilities to others.

On the road, jumping from city to city, university to university, airport to airport, she was often asked to visit the chimpanzees at the zoos, and in so doing she came upon an idea:

"I suddenly realized the exciting potential of these invaluable captive groups. If only, I thought, we could collect comparable data at a number of different zoo sites, using the same behavior categories as we do at Gombe, and similar recording techniques, a whole wealth of new information would soon become available. We would gradually learn more about the extent to which chimpanzee behavior is flexible. In how many ways do chimpanzees adapt to the different social and physical environments? It would give us a chance to tap the vast store of knowledge and expertise so often stored away in the heads of individual keepers. And it would also lead to better environments for the chimpanzees."

ChimpanZoo, as the program is called, came into being in 1984 with six participating zoos, all eager to contribute to Jane's data collection on chimpanzees—both wild and in captivity. And, more importantly, they saw the need, through her eyes, to improve the environments of the chimpanzees in their care.

ABOVE: *If not rescued, young Kipara—a resident of the Kitwe Point sanctuary—would have met with a cruel fate.* OPPOSITE: *Jane feeds a dehydrated chimp that she found for sale on the streets of Kinshasa, Zaire. The selling of chimpanzees is illegal in most range countries across the African continent, and Jane has been an impassioned public voice for the enforcement of the law.*

"There are not many people who, after meeting an orphaned infant and looking into those desperate eyes, can turn away."

CHIMPANZOO

Founded in 1984, ChimpanZoo is an international research program dedicated to the study of chimpanzees in zoos and other captive settings. Approximately 130 chimpanzees are involved in ChimpanZoo, making it the largest captive ape research program ever undertaken. Trained by participating zoos and the Jane Goodall Institute, students, caretakers, and volunteers record behavioral observations and work with zoo keepers to improve the lives of captive chimpanzees and compare their behavior to that of chimps in the wild.

The results of the studies are presented at an annual, week-long ChimpanZoo conference, the location of which changes each year. It serves as a forum for discussing and exchanging new information and ideas. The conference attracts the academic and zoological communities, as well as the general public. Guest lecturers are also invited to speak about their latest research, and findings are published in scholarly journals. The database is also accessible to zoos, students, and instructors.

THE GOALS OF CHIMPANZOO

- **Increase public awareness about the plight of chimpanzees and increase understanding of chimpanzee behavior.**

- **Assist zoos in their efforts to improve the habitats and conditions for captive chimpanzees.**

- **Facilitate the exchange of information on ways to enrich the lives of captive chimpanzees.**

- **Compile behavioral data for an international database.**

ABOVE AND OPPOSITE: *Chimpanzees in the wild have the freedom to play in the trees or relax on the ground.*
The same is not true for many captive chimps, who must endure lives spent in small enclosures.

THE TIME LINE

MAY 25, 1988
JGI-UK IS ESTABLISHED IN LONDON WITH THE FIRST MEETING OF THE BOARD OF TRUSTEES.

1988
JANE RECEIVES THE CENTENNIAL AWARD FROM THE NATIONAL GEOGRAPHIC SOCIETY IN WASHINGTON, DC.

SPRING 1990
WILKIE DEFEATS GOBLIN, WHOSE REIGN LASTED NINE YEARS, TO BECOME THE ALPHA MALE AT GOMBE.

JULY 1990
JGI-TANZANIA IS LAUNCHED IN CON-JUNCTION WITH JANE GOODALL'S GOMBE 30 CELEBRATION — OBSERVING THIRTY YEARS SINCE SHE FIRST BEGAN HER RESEARCH IN TANZANIA.

1990
CHIMPS, SO LIKE US, AN HBO DOCUMENTARY, IS PRODUCED. THE FILM IS NOMINATED FOR AN ACADEMY AWARD.

As Jane became more interested in the proper care of chimpanzees living in zoos, she became aware of a much more grave condition in which chimpanzees were living: medical laboratories. Though she could imagine the horrors these innocent creatures lived through each day in the cold, sometimes solitary, cages of the research buildings, she could not comment until she saw the conditions for herself. In 1987, she visited her first medical research facility, and later wrote about the experience in Britain's *Sunday Times*:

"Room after room was lined with small, bare cages, stacked one above the other, in which monkeys circled round and round, and chimpanzees sat huddled, far gone in depression and despair.

"Young chimpanzees, three or four years old, were crammed, two together, into tiny cages measuring 22 inches by 22 inches and only 24 inches high. They could hardly turn around.

"The chimps had each other for comfort, but they would not be together for long. Once they are infected, probably with hepatitis, they will be separated and placed in another cage. And there they will remain, living in conditions of severe sensory deprivation, for the next several years. During that time, they will become insane.

ABOVE: *This deformed and abused chimpanzee lays in his small cage at a bio-medical laboratory. Jane had avoided visiting such facilities for a time, feeling there would be nothing she could do to help. Now she is one of the leading advocates for the abolition of the use of all live animals in research and, until then, the humane treatment of research animals.* OPPOSITE: *Jane comforts a young chimp that serves as a living prop for a beach photographer in the Canary Islands.*

"If we shouldn't do something to humans, should we do it to chimps?"

"A juvenile female rocked side to side, sealed off from the outside world behind the glass doors of her metal isolation chamber. She was in semidarkness. All she could hear was the incessant roar of air rushing through vents into her prison.

"I shall be haunted forever by her eyes, and the eyes of the other chimpanzees I saw that day.

"I have had the privilege of working among wild, free chimpanzees for more than twenty-six years. I have gained a deep understanding of chimpanzee nature. Chimpanzees have given me so much in my life. The least I can do is speak out for the hundreds of chimpanzees who, right now, sit hunched, miserable and without hope, staring out with dead eyes from their metal prisons. They cannot speak for themselves."

And so she did. Jane spoke with people from the National Institutes of Health. She spoke with the directors of laboratories that housed chimpanzees. She spoke with senators and members of congress. She soon found out that the lab she visited was one of the worst, that others had larger cages or group housing. But she fought to have the regulations changed, so all labs were required to treat the chimpanzees humanely. Knowing how the chimpanzees lived in the wild, she knew that the conditions in which they were kept were sorely inadequate. She worked with others to write recommendations on more humane care, larger cages, and enriched environments.

Jane also began to speak out on behalf of captive chimps in Africa. She had heard of the many chimpanzees kept as pets in the homes of wealthy foreigners, or offered for sale at village markets. But she had never seen one of these unfortunate individuals until 1990, when she gazed into the eyes of Gregoire—a hairless chimpanzee who had been imprisoned in a lonely steel cage in a Brazzaville Zoo since 1940—and saw first-hand a tiny, frightened orphan, stolen from the forest by poachers.

"For years I have talked about the pitiful plight of infant chimpanzees who are sold in native markets. Now I have seen this with my own eyes. He was about one and a half years old, tied, by a short piece of rope, on the top of a chicken mesh [cage]. The trees overhead cast a little shade, but it was swelteringly hot and he was apathetic, dehydrated and sweating. When I bent over him, he reached a gentle hand to touch my face. It is

ABOVE: *Jane reaches out to her old friend Gregoire, whom she discovered living in wretched conditions in a Congolese zoo and who now resides at the Institute's Tchimpounga sanctuary.*

"I shall never forget my first sight of Gregoire in the Brazzaville zoo in Congo. Emaciated, hairless and crazed, he looked like a being out of Belsen or Auschwitz. He had lived in that bleak, dark cage, alone since 1944-how, for heaven's sake, how had he clung to life?"

"**D**uring my first visit to Brazzaville Zoo in Congo, I met Gregoire. I can still recall my sense of disbelief and outrage as I gazed at this strange being, alone in his bleak cement-floored cage. His pale, almost hairless skin was stretched tighly over his emaciated body so that every bone could be seen. His eyes were dull as he reached out with a thin, bony hand for a proffered morsel of food. Was this really a chimpanzee? Apparently so. Above his cage was a sign that read 'Shimpanse— 1944.' 1944! It was hard to believe. In that dim, unfriendly cage, Gregoire had endured for forty-six years!

"A group of Congolese children approached him quietly. One girl, about ten years old, had a banana in her hand. Leaning over the safety rail, she called out, 'Danse! Gregoire—Danse!' With bizarre, stereotyped movements, the old male stood upright and twirled around three times. Then, still standing, he drummed rapidly with his hands on a single piece of furniture in his room, a lopsided shelf attached to one wall. He ended the strange performance by standing on his hands, his feet gripping the bars between us. The girl held the banana toward him and, righting himself, he reached out to accept his payment.

"That meeting was just after Nelson Mandela had been released from his long imprisonment by the white South African government. I was with a Congolese official at the time, who knew nothing of chimpanzees. After staring at Gregoire for a while he turned to me, his face solemn. 'There, I think, is our Mandela,' he said. I was moved by those words, by the compassion that lay behind them.

The gaunt image of Gregoire hung between me and sleep that night. How had he survived those long, weary years deprived of almost everything that a chimpanzee needs to make life meaningful? What stubbornness of spirit had kept him alive? It was as though he, like other starving, neglected chimpanzees in impoverished African zoos, had been waiting for help."

At Jane's insistence, the Jane Goodall Institute hired a Congolese worker to look after Gregoire—to provide him with nourishment. Soon, his barren cage was expanded to include a small outdoor "deck" and he began to grow hair and put on weight. In late 1996, Gregoire was introduced to a four-year-old male orphan named Bobby and an infant female, whom Jane named Cheri. Despite the fifty-year age difference, Bobby and Gregoire play together like children. And the old male treats young Cheri like a much loved granddaughter.

In May 1997, civil war broke out in Congo. Fortunately, a team of wildlife experts rescued the great apes of the Brazzaville Zoo and moved them to safety. Gregoire and his companions are now living at the Institute's Tchimpounga sanctuary near Pointe-Noire, where Cheri sleeps each night in the circle of Gregoire's arms.

"Gregoire has survived capture, three decades of solitary confinement, starvation, and two revolutions. Finally, in his old age, he has found love."

not legal to sell chimpanzees in this way in Zaire—not without all the proper permits. Yet he was brazenly exhibited right outside the American Cultural Center [in Kinshasa, Zaire]. We knew we could not leave him there. Nor could we buy him, thus encouraging the trade."

This young chimpanzee, named Little Jay, was to launch yet another arm of the Jane Goodall Institute. Because it is illegal to sell chimpanzees in most African range countries, Jane's first step was to encourage the governments to enforce their laws. To do this, government officials must confiscate the chimpanzees, showing the poachers and traders that there is no money to be made in this illegal venture. But once the governments have the chimpanzees in their custody, the chimpanzees need someplace to go. They cannot be returned to the wild because they lack the skills they would need to survive— skills they would have learned from their mothers. Chimpanzees are also very social within their communities, but territorial when dealing with outsiders. A lone chimpanzee placed in a unfamiliar forest would surely be killed.

The solution, therefore, was to provide a safe haven, a sanctuary, for these chimpanzees to live out their lives in peace—in the company of other chimpanzees. With the assistance of Dan Phillips, United States ambassador, and his wife Lucie, the first

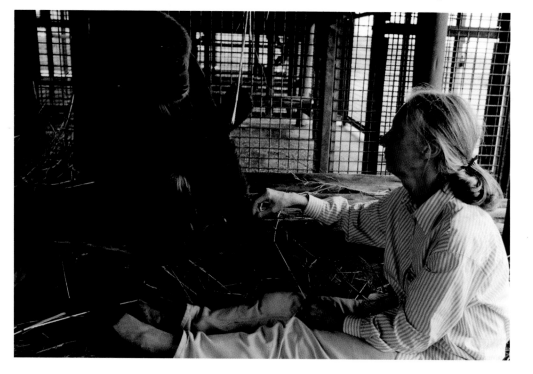

Jane Goodall Institute sanctuary was established in Burundi, a small Central African country north of Tanzania and on the border of Zaire (now Congo). Although Burundi has a small population of chimpanzees in their northern and southern patches of forest, many of the pet chimpanzees living throughout Burundi were actually smuggled across the border from Zaire. The chimpanzees, who grew in number to twenty, never left the so-called "halfway house" in the capital city of Bujumbura, because the political instability of this troubled country continued to put sanctuary plans on hold. In 1995, the Institute transferred the chimpanzees

ABOVE: *A young chimp is bottle-fed formula. Many of the orphans are severely malnourished when they arrive at the sanctuaries, and must be hand-fed until they are able to hold a cup on their own.* OPPOSITE: *Jane spends a private moment with La Vieille, an aged female chimpanzee half crazed from spending years caged alone in a Congolese zoo. The Institute moved La Vieille to the Tchimpounga sanctuary in Pointe-Noire in 1994.*

to 200 acres of riverine woodland in central Kenya, near the foot of Mt. Kenya. Although chimpanzees are not indigenous to Kenya, these chimpanzees at last can climb trees, build nests, and rest in the warm African sun, free of chains and bars.

The largest of the JGI sanctuaries opened in 1992 in Pointe-Noire, Congo, with the generous help of Conoco Inc. The sanctuary, which sits on a forested area of about 100 hectares, is now home to more than fifty chimpanzees, ranging in age from less than one year to old Gregoire, now at least fifty-five years old, who was transferred to the sanctuary from the Brazzaville Zoo in 1997.

Kitwe Point sanctuary, located about 14 miles south of Gombe National Park in the town of Kigoma, Tanzania, houses three male chimpanzees—the lone survivors of a group of six discovered in a crate bound for the airport in 1995, and confiscated by the Tanzanian authorities from Zaire poachers.

And nineteen chimpanzees—former pets and residents of zoos, along with four chimpanzees that were stolen from the Entebbe Zoo and smuggled all the way to Hungary before their rescue and return—live on Ngamba Island, 100 acres of rainforest paradise in Lake Victoria near Entebbe, Uganda.

The hunting and selling of chimpanzees, for meat and for pets, continues throughout Africa. For every infant chimpanzee rescued and brought to the doorstep of a JGI sanctuary, at least ten others may have died during the capture. And because Jane cannot forget that tiny, gentle hand that touched her face in the market that day—and the countless orphaned hands she has touched since—she is committed to putting this practice to an end. With the orphaned chimpanzees as ambassadors, each sanctuary also operates an environmental education and conservation program for the local people, encouraging elders and children alike to appreciate and value their surrounding forests and the animals who live there.

At the chimpanzee sanctuary at Ngamba Island, Uganda, a female chimpanzee rests comfortably after an active day in the forest.

ABOVE: *On Ngamba Island, chimps have the freedom to roam and sit in the tall grass just as they would in the wild.* OPPOSITE: *Young chimps—like these at Tchimpounga—arrive at the sanctuaries severely traumatized from the loss of their mothers, yet they show remarkable resiliency in forming companion relationships that will last their lifetime.*

"If only we could overcome cruelty with compassion
we should make a gigantic stride toward achieving
our ultimate human potential, moving beyond the
Age of Reason to the Age of Love."

Kitwe Point Sanctuary

ABOVE: *Felicia Nutter, a caretaker at Kitwe Point, cradles an orphaned chimp.* OPPOSITE: *Removed from their communities, chimpanzees at the sanctuaries form new bonds. Although each sanctuary is a controlled environment, it is the most natural world in which these chimpanzees will ever survive.*

In 1994, Tanzania authorities confiscated a group of six young chimpanzees that had been smuggled from eastern Zaire. The rescued chimps were cared for by Institute staff in temporary facilities at the Aqua Lodge in Kigoma.

In late 1995, the Kitwe Point Sanctuary was established and the chimpanzees were moved to their current home. The sanctuary is situated on a 6-acre peninsula jutting out into Lake Tanganiyka, just south of Kigoma, about 14 miles south of Gombe National Park. Only three chimpanzees—all males—remain of the original six: Dosi, Kipara, and Zorro.

The sanctuary is within a larger area of forest reserve, all of which is now under the management of JGI-Tanzania's TACARE project (see page 110). As the chimps grew older, the original fence across the neck of the peninsula was no longer adequate to keep them in, making it unsafe for school children or tourists to visit. With the help of experts from Monkey World in the United Kingdom, and the efforts of volunteers and the hard-working Tanzanian staff, a new fence was erected in November 1998.

Tchimpounga Sanctuary

Tchimpounga was established near Pointe-Noire in the Congo Republic in December 1992 with the support of Conoco Inc. Tchimpounga is run by a remarkable woman named Graziella Cotman, who fled Zaire with Little Jay and other orphaned chimps in the early 1990s. Her dedication has been many chimps' only hope for survival amid Congo's civil wars and ongoing political strife. The sanctuary is surrounded by electric fencing and includes spacious caging (where the chimpanzees spend the night and sick chimps or new arrivals are cared for), a large savanna area, and an area of thick rainforest where the chimps spend most of their day.

The success of rescue efforts has stretched Tchimpounga to maximum capacity. An escalation of the bush-meat trade supplies an ever-increasing population of orphans: since small infants have little meat, the hunters will try to sell them as pets and the government has cooperated greatly in confiscating these orphans. They come to the sanctuary from Congo-Zaire and Gabon, as well as from Congo-Brazzaville itself. There are now fifty-five chimpanzees living at Tchimpounga and new enclosures are urgently needed.

In cooperation with the government, JGI-Congo is developing a beautiful stretch of forest-savanna mosaic as a wildlife reserve that will surround the sanctuary and hopefully save the natural habitat of the wild chimpanzees that remain in the area.

School children and other Pointe-Noire residents visit the sanctuary regularly, and it is hoped that—with political stability—an overseas tourism program can be developed to bring much-needed foreign exchange into the country.

ABOVE: *An aerial view of the Tchimpounga facility, which features a large area of forest as well as grasslands for its residents.*
OPPOSITE: *Sanctuary chimps reside in spacious cages at night, and the facilities are also used to house new arrivals and sick chimpanzees.*

PAGES 92–95: *Each morning, caretakers at Tchimpounga ensure that the chimpanzees are well fed before they are led to the forest for the day. The older chimps will wait their turn for food until the youngsters are cared for.*

Playmates frolic around caretaker Ludovic Rabasa, who doubles as a surrogate parent to the orphans at Tchimpounga sanctuary. Like human children, young chimpanzees learn much of their behavior from adults. In the sanctuaries, the human caretakers must often fulfill the role of "teaching" orphaned chimps.

Uganda

ABOVE: *A ranger at the Kibale Rain Forest Visitor's Center—a companion project to the sanctuary—teaches a group of visiting school children about the dangers of snares. The snares are placed illegally by poachers to capture animals for sale in the bush-meat trade. Although chimpanzees may have the strength to break the wire, they cannot remove the snare, and are left badly injured.* OPPOSITE: *Stani, a caretaker at Ngamba Island, Uganda, carries a young chimp.*

In October 1998, the JGI-Uganda sanctuary took an important step forward in providing the orphaned chimpanzees with a beautiful and safe living environment. Nineteen chimps from the Isinga Island sanctuary and the Entebbe Wildlife Education Centre were successfully relocated to the much larger Ngamba Island sanctuary on Lake Victoria. All of the chimpanzees are adjusting well to their new home and to their new companions.

JGI-Uganda, under the direction of Linda Rothen and Debby Cox, is also working with the government to protect the wild chimpanzee populations throughout the country, with eco-tourism, snare removal, and environmental education.

ABOVE: *A portrait of Max, one of the residents at the Sweetwaters sanctuary.*

OPPOSITE: *Jane spends a quiet moment with Freud at Gombe. Her efforts on behalf of chimps worldwide stem from the gratitude she feels toward the communities at Gombe.*

Sweetwaters Sanctuary

The Sweetwaters Sanctuary was built by Lonrho Corp. in close collaboration with JGI in 1993. It is situated inside the 23,000-acre Sweetwaters Game Reserve near Nanyuki, Kenya. Originally established as a black rhino breeding sanctuary, it now has a great variety of wildlife and attracts much tourism.

Chimpanzees are not indigenous to Kenya; the sanctuary was established to provide shelter and care for orphaned chimpanzees rescued from other areas. In 1994, due to the unstable political situation in the central African nation of Burundi, the Jane Goodall Institute requested and received permission from the Burundian and Kenyan governments to relocate the twenty chimpanzees from JGI's Halfway House in Bujumbura, Burundi, to Kenya.

These orphans had mostly originated in eastern Zaire. They have settled in well at their new home, and now live in two large groups. A few other orphans have been introduced to the communities since the relocation.

The sanctuary, run by Annie Olivecrona, has excellent facilities for observation and provides visual access for education and observational studies conducted by school children, primatologists, anthropologists, and others interested in chimpanzee behavior.

The People

"Every individual matters. Every individual has a role to play. Every individual makes a difference."

Through Jane Goodall's work with chimpanzees we learned that humans are not as different from the rest of the animal world as we once thought, that we are not the only beings capable of rational thought, of emotions, and of mental and physical suffering.

This realization led Jane to yet another discovery: once we begin to accept that animals do indeed suffer, we must begin to scrutinize the way in which we treat all animals, human and nonhuman alike, as well as the environment in which they live.

In celebration of thirty years of research, Jane invited a select group of students to her house in Dar es Salaam, Tanzania. "How do you feel when you see chickens carried upside down?" Jane asked the students gathered around her verandah. She was referring to the common practice in Tanzania of carrying live chickens by their legs to and from the market, as they hang upside down squawking and flapping their wings to get free. The students' answers were to launch Jane Goodall's most cherished project to date: an international coalition of young people who care about the earth.

"I do have hope for the future of our planet, but that hope is dependent not only on policy change in business and industry, but on huge numbers of people waking up to the danger and realizing that each of us has a role to play.... This is the message I want to share with people—especially children—around the world."

The students responded with compassion. Although the chicken is going to die, to become someone's supper, they replied, while the animal still lives we should treat it with respect.

This is the answer Jane sought, a recognition that every individual matters, human and nonhuman alike, and that every individual deserves our respect and compassion. These fifteen students pledged to Jane and to each other that they would strive to make the world a better place, to conserve the natural environment and improve conditions for wild and domestic animals. And they pledged to share this mission with those around them.

Through the enthusiasm of these first students, more than thirty clubs have now been started in primary and secondary schools throughout Dar es Salaam and many other parts of Tanzania. Jane saw the energy in these young people, the potential, and the hope. She saw that attitudes and generations-old practices could change through the strength of the world's children. In 1991, Roots & Shoots was born.

> "Roots creep underground and make a firm foundation
> Shoots seem very weak, but to reach the light they can break open brick walls.
> Imagine that the brick walls are all the problems we have inflicted on our planet.
> Hundreds and thousands of roots and shoots,
> Hundreds and thousands of young people around the world,
> Can break through these walls.
> Together, we can change the world."

Today there are Roots & Shoots groups in more than fifty countries, with at least 1,100 groups in the United States alone. With the goal of teaching young people (from kindergarten to university) the interconnectedness and interdependence of life, Jane Goodall's Roots & Shoots program encourages groups to show care and compassion for animals, for the environment, and for each other through cooperative, hands-on projects. Across the globe, Roots & Shoots groups do their part to make the world, and their community, a better place—from cleaning a stream in Oregon to planting a tree in Tanzania, walking a neighbor's dog in Minnesota to visiting a hospital in South Africa.

"I think Roots & Shoots is probably the reason I came into the world. Yet I couldn't have done it without all those years with the chimpanzees and an understanding that

OPPOSITE: Jane visits Roots & Shoots programs taking place in schools around the world, speaking with the children and learning about the projects they are working on to help the environment.

THE TIME LINE

1993
**Visions of Calaban:
On Chimpanzees and People**
is published, written by Jane
and Dale Peterson.

1994
After a Mitumba chimp joined
the Kasekela group, Flossi,
daughter of Fifi, suddenly
begins using the Mitumba tech-
nique of catching carpenter
ants with twigs. It is the first
observation of technology
transfer from one community
of chimpanzees to another.

1995
Jane receives the National
Geographic Society's Hubbard
Medal for distinction in
exploration, discovery,
and research. The award is
presented to her by Vice
President Al Gore.

1995
Jane is awarded the status of
CBE (Commander of the British
Empire) by H.M. Queen Elizabeth II.

February 1995
Rafiki, in Gombe's Mitumba community, gives birth to twins,
whom Jane names Roots and
Shoots. They are only the second set of twins known to have
been observed at Gombe.

led to a blurring of the line between 'man' and 'beast.' Children give me particular hope because they have more open minds. They aren't as set in their ways. Only if children grow up with respect for all living things will the planet have a chance for survival."

Nowhere is this more apparent to Jane than in Tanzania, home of Gombe Stream National Park—her haven from the stress and chaos of life on the road. But Gombe itself is under siege from the growing village populations that surround it on three sides. The lush green forest stands out like a tiny island amid the barren hills, the trees long ago cut by villagers in search of virgin soil for cultivation, fuel wood and building materials. The precious top soil has washed down the steep hills into the lake, stripping the ground of fertility and polluting the once-clear waters with red mud.

The destructive farming practices used by the villagers in the Kigoma region around Gombe force the women to inch ever closer to the virgin forest in search of land for their meager crops—giving this region the second highest annual rate of deforestation in all of Tanzania. Refugees from neighboring Burundi and Congo-Zaire add to the already dense population, bringing additional pressure on the scant resources. The Kigoma region has a 20 percent infant mortality rate and is the second poorest region in all of Tanzania.

How do you save a precious 30 square miles of forest, Jane asked herself, when the people around it are facing starvation? Once again acting on her adage that every individual matters, she devised a plan. With the help of professionals in the field of natural resource management and community development, she founded the Lake Tanganyika Catchment Reforestation and Education (TACARE) project. The founders' initial goal was to arrest the degradation and erosion of land in the Kigoma region through improved farming and agroforesty methods that would benefit the people and take pressure off the Gombe forest.

In 1993, under the direction of project director George Strunden, the Jane Goodall Institute launched the first phase of TACARE tree nurseries in twenty-nine villages—tiny communities of crude mud houses and thatch roofs, where water is often a five-hour walk away, and dinner is prepared over a small wood fire. TACARE provided

OPPOSITE: *This young girl is planting a tree as part of a Roots & Shoots project in Kigoma, Tanzania.*

ABOUT ROOT & SHOOTS

The Jane Goodall Institute established Roots & Shoots, an environmental education and humanitarian program for youth, in Dar es Salaam, Tanzania, in 1991. The program was developed with the goal of empowering young people to coordinate constructive service projects in their own communities. Through locally based projects, Roots & Shoots focuses on hands-on learning, global networking, and constructive action.

Roots & Shoots members include preschool- to university-level youth in schools and community groups around the world. There are currently registered groups in more than fifty countries, with groups in forty-four states in the United States. Roots & Shoots emphasizes cross-cultural interaction and enables young people to continue to coordinate projects locally that promote care and concern for the environment, animals, and human communities.

Through constructive activities the participants of Roots & Shoots groups all over the world become more aware of how their actions affect their local community and the environment as a whole.

Registered groups receive a number of benefits, including newsletters and reports from the Institute, eligibility to participate in the Roots & Shoots North American Youth and College Summits, and the Dr. Jane Goodall/Roots & Shoots Achievement Awards Program.

Most importantly, these groups are part of a global youth network, Partnerships in Understanding, that provides opportunities for groups around the world to share ideas, solve problems, and enhance cultural awareness.

ABOVE: *Jane reaches out to children throughout the world and from all parts of society.*
Here, she speaks with a homeless child in Dar es Salaam, Tanzania. OPPOSITE: *This group*
of middle-school students in Danbury, Connecticut, has created artwork as part of the Roots
& Shoots program at their school.

THE TIME LINE

1995

PNEUMONIA STRIKES THE MITUMBA GROUP, KILLING ABOUT ONE THIRD OF THE POPULATION. RAFIKI AND HER YOUNG TWINS, ROOTS AND SHOOTS, ARE THREE OF THE VICTIMS.

1996

JANE RECEIVES THE TANZANIAN KILIMANJARO MEDAL, PRESENTED BY PRESIDENT MWINYI, FOR HER CONTRIBUTIONS TO WILDLIFE CONSERVATION.

SUMMER 1997

MANGE, A SKIN DISEASE, INFILTRATES THE KASEKELA COMMUNITY, HITTING HARDEST ON THE NURSING FEMALES AND THEIR INFANTS. FIFI LOSES HER INFANT SON, FRED. ALSO AFFECTED ARE FREUD, PROF, GOBLIN, AND BEETHOVEN.

OCTOBER 2, 1997

FRODO OVERTHROWS HIS AILING BROTHER FREUD AS THE ALPHA MALE OF THE KASEKELA GROUP.

JULY 1998

GREMLIN GIVES BIRTH TO GOMBE'S NEWEST SET OF TWINS, GOLDEN AND GLITTA. FIFI GIVES BIRTH TO HER THIRD DAUGHTER, FLIRT.

1999

JANE'S EIGHTH BOOK, **REASON FOR HOPE: A SPIRITUAL JOURNEY**, IS PUBLISHED.

seedlings to each nursery, based on the needs and desires of the community—vegetables, fruit trees, firewood, and cash crops like oil palm trees, coconut, and coffee.

Each village was assigned a village leader as the nursery attendant, who would distribute seedlings to the rest of the community, and organize seminars by TACARE staff in proper planting and care, contour farming, and water and soil conservation.

Led by director George Strunden and education coordinator Emmanuel Mtiti, the TACARE staff, most of them native Tanzanians trained in agroforesty, focused their program on the women of Kigoma—traditionally responsible for farming, food preparation, and gathering of firewood while their husbands fish for dagaa on the nearby lake.

Jane also introduced her Roots & Shoots program to the local primary and secondary schools, to instill in the children a love and appreciation for their environment and a desire to try to save it. They, too, have tree nurseries, where they learn, as children, environmentally sustainable farming practices.

TACARE broadened to support private women's tree nurseries, school tree nurseries, health care, and even small loan programs to help women start their own businesses. Lucy Hamenya, 35, mother of five, is a founding member of one of the first TACARE women's groups in the Kagongo village. As she bends down to pull weeds from the plants in the group's thriving nursery, with the bare hills surrounding Gombe as a backdrop, she explains the name the women chose for their group. "We called it *Matumaini* [hope] because we have hope we will one day succeed. That one day we will harvest, and make our economy better than today."

The TACARE project is supported, in part, by the European Union Community, and is attracting other international development organizations because of its success.

OPPOSITE: *This young woman participates in the TACARE project in Kigoma, Tanzania.*

ABOUT TACARE

TACARE project manager George Strunden works with an outstanding team of Tanzanians, headed by Emmanuel Mtiti, who have helped make TACARE a success.

The shocking deforestation seen along the eastern shore of Lake Tanganyika from Kigoma to the Burundi border (and beyond) crept up on people without warning. Suddenly, it seemed, the trees were gone. The Kigoma region of western Tanzania has the second highest yearly deforestation rate in the country. The addition of thousands of refugees from Burundi and Zaire (now the Democratic Republic of Congo), along with the rapidly growing local population, has put an insupportable demand on the natural resources, as forests are cleared for farming, building, and domestic uses.

The Jane Goodall Institute established the Lake Tanganyika Catchment Reforestation and Education project (TACARE) in October 1994 to provide alternate and improved means of survival for people who live on the margins of the forest. Through education, assistance, health care, and support, TACARE helps women of the Kigoma region provide a better future for their families—and, in turn, a more promising future for the environment.

THE GOALS OF TACARE

• Arrest the rapid degradation of land in the Kigoma region.

• Improve the standard of living of the villagers by providing training and resources for growing fruit trees and vegetables.

• Promote reforestation.

• Curb soil erosion.

• Provide conservation education to the local population.

• Improve skills, education, and self-esteem of women.

• Provide primary health care, AIDS education, and family planning services, in cooperation with the regional medical offices.

"Our efforts to involve local citizens in restoring the forests and practicing sustainable agriculture is the most important work that we can do to ensure a future for the Gombe chimpanzees and the people of Africa. And that is why we started TACARE."

ABOVE: *In the Kigoma region, it is typical for the women to tend to farming and caring for the family while the men spend their time fishing from Lake Tanganyika. TACARE staff provide education, training, and supplies to promote the growth of crops that will aid in the development of a sustainable economy.* OPPOSITE: *A woman waters plants in one of the women's group tree nurseries in the Kigoma region. The women buy the seedlings from TACARE and receive training in proper care and management of their investments.*

OPPOSITE AND ABOVE LEFT: *TACARE works with the local communities in western Tanzania on improved farming techniques, especially of such cash crops as oil palm seeds, shown here. In progress is a hybridization program that should result in a crop of oil palm seeds with a potential four-time increase of oil per seed.* LEFT: *Beans are hung from a roof to dry.*

ABOVE: *TACARE is concerned with a wide range of environmental concerns. This woman is using a fuel-saving stove, as she was taught by TACARE staff.* OPPOSITE: *Women and children carry water from great distances to use for cooking and watering their crops.*

"I spend as much time as possible with the
chimps. Those precious times serve to recharge my
batteries and give me the strength for all the
other things I have to do today."

The Promise

ABOVE: *Jane sits with her dog, Wiski-Biski, near Bournmouth, England.* OPPOSITE: *Back at Gombe, Jane sits with Fifi's son, Freud.*

Since 1986, Jane Goodall has not stayed in any one place longer than three weeks. When not in Africa or her home in England, her days are spent on airplanes, traveling to speaking engagements, receptions, press conferences, and lobbying for environmental causes. It was difficult for Jane to leave her paradise at Gombe, but now she is in constant motion, knowing that she has important work to do. Jane has seen much of man's inhumanity, our senseless destruction of the natural world and our own cruelty—to humans and non-humans alike. Yet she maintains a sense of hope for the future.

"As we move toward the millennium, it is easy to be overwhelmed by feelings of hopelessness. We humans have destroyed the balance of nature: forests are being destroyed, deserts are spreading, there is terrible pollution and poisoning of air, earth, water. Climate is changing, people are starving. There are too many humans in some parts of the world, overconsumption in others. There is human cruelty to 'man' and 'beast' alike; there is violence and war. Yet I do have hope. Let me share my four reasons.

"Firstly, we have at last begun to understand and face up to the problems that threaten the survival of life on earth. And we are problem-solving creatures. Our amazing brains have

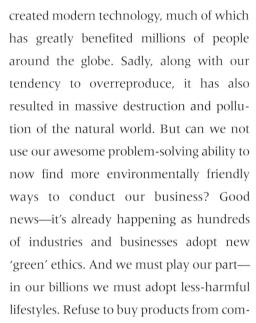

created modern technology, much of which has greatly benefited millions of people around the globe. Sadly, along with our tendency to overreproduce, it has also resulted in massive destruction and pollution of the natural world. But can we not use our awesome problem-solving ability to now find more environmentally friendly ways to conduct our business? Good news—it's already happening as hundreds of industries and businesses adopt new 'green' ethics. And we must play our part— in our billions we must adopt less-harmful lifestyles. Refuse to buy products from companies, corporations, that do not confirm to new environmental standards, We *can* change the world.

"Second, nature is amazingly resilient. Given the chance, poisoned rivers can live again. Deforested land can be coaxed—or left—to blossom again. Animal species, on the verge of extinction, can sometimes be bred and saved from a few individuals.

"My third reason for hope lies in the tremendous energy, enthusiasm, and commitment of young people around the world. Young people want to fight to right the wrongs, for it will be their world tomorrow—they will be the ones in leadership positions, and they themselves will be parents....

"My fourth reason for hope lies in the indomitable nature of the human spirit. There are so many people who have dreamed seemingly unattainable dreams and, because they never gave up, achieved their goals against all the odds, or blazed a path along which others could follow.

"So let us move into the next millennium with hope—with faith in ourselves, in our intellect, in our indomitable spirit. Let us develop respect for all living things. Let us try to replace violence and intolerance with understanding and compassion. And love."

"I often have problems sleeping. I suppose I'm trying to do too many things. Once I let go, it all comes crowding in and I have pictures in my mind of chimps in chains, chimps in laboratories. It's awful. It colors my watching the wild chimps. I think, 'Aren't they lucky?' and then think about other tiny chimps in tiny prisons, though they have committed no crimes. Once you've seen it, you can't forget."

The Jane Goodall Institute is a tax-exempt, nonprofit organization founded in 1977. The Institute was initially formed to provide ongoing support for field research on wild chimpanzees and to help arrest the rapid decline of chimpanzee populations in the wild and neglect and abuse in captivity.

Under Jane Goodall's direction, the Institute has expanded its mission—to bring together common efforts in education, community development, conservation, and humanitarianism to make the world a better place.

THE JANE GOODALL INSTITUTE'S PROJECTS ARE:

Roots & Shoots, an environmental and humanitarian education program for young people from kindergarten to university level, encouraging all people to take action to show care and concern for animals, the environment and their own community.

TACARE, a reforestation and community development project in western Tanzania, focused on improving the residents' standard of living while promoting reforestation, curbing soil erosion, and expanding conservation education for the local population.

ChimpanZoo, an international research program dedicated to the behavioral study of chimpanzees in zoos and other captive settings and the improvement of their living conditions.

HOW YOU CAN HELP

You can support Jane Goodall in her efforts to make the world a better place:

• Become a member of the Jane Goodall Institute

• Start or join a Roots & Shoots group in your school or community

• Become a guardian to a chimpanzee in a JGI sanctuary

THE MISSION OF THE JANE GOODALL INSTITUTE IS TO ADVANCE THE POWER OF INDIVIDUALS TO TAKE INFORMED AND COMPASSIONATE ACTION TO IMPROVE THE ENVIRONMENT OF ALL LIVING THINGS.

Sanctuaries, providing long-term care and rehabilitation for chimpanzees orphaned by poachers and working with governments to curb poaching of chimpanzees for the pet and bushmeat trades.

Gombe Stream Research Centre, where Goodall and her staff of researchers continue to contribute significant findings on chimpanzee behavior. The long-term study of Gombe's baboons began in 1967.

PUBLICATIONS:

The Jane Goodall Institute World Report Newsletter (*annual*)

The Roots & Shoots Network Newsletter (*semi-annual*)

The ChimpanZoo Newsletter (*annual*)

Website: www.janegoodall.org

FOR MORE INFORMATION, CONTACT THE JANE GOODALL INSTITUTE OFFICE NEAREST YOU, OR VISIT THEIR WEBSITE: WWW.JANEGOODALL.ORG

124

THE JANE GOODALL INSTITUTE

JGI-USA
PO Box 14890
Silver Spring, MD 20911-4890
fax (301) 565-3188
www.janegoodall.org

JGI-Austria
Bonauweg 11
A05020 Salzburg
Austria

JGI-Canada
PO Box 477
Victoria Station
Westmount, Quebec
H3Z 2Y6 Canada
e-mail: janegoodall@jonction.net

JGI-Germany
Herzogstrasse 60
D-80803 Muenchen
Germany
e-mail: jgoodall@compuserve.com

JGI-Holland
Postbus 61
7213 ZH Gorssel
The Netherlands

JGI-South Africa
PO Box 87527
Houghton 2047
South Africa

JGI-Tanzania
PO Box 727
Dar es Salaam
Tanzania

JGI-ROC
2/F no. 43, Section 2
Hin-Hai Road
Taipei, Taiwan

JGI-UK
15 Clarendon Park
Lymington, Hants
SO41 8AX
England

JGI-Uganda
PO Box 4187
Kampala, Uganda

Kitwe Point Sanctuary
PO Box 767
Kigoma, Tanzania

Tchimpounga Sanctuary
JGI-Congo
BP 1893
Pointe-Noire, Congo

Sweetwaters
Chimpanzee Sanctuary
PO Box 167
Nanyuki, Kenya

Ngamba Island
Chimpanzee Sanctuary
JGI-Uganda
PO Box 360
Entebbe, Uganda

ChimpanZoo
Dr. Virginia Landau
Director of ChimpanZoo
800 East University Blvd.
Geronimo Building,
Room #308
Tucson, AZ 85721

Roots & Shoots
The Jane Goodall Institute
PO Box 14890
Silver Spring, MD 20911
fax (301) 565-3188

TACARE
George Stranden
PO Box 1182
Kigoma, Tanzania

PHOTO CREDITS

Page 1: photo by Stephen Patch, courtesy JGI. **Pages 2–3:** photo © Michael Neugebauer. **Page 5:** photo © Michael Nichols. **Pages 6–7:** photo © Michael Neugebauer. **Page 8:** photo by Chris Boehm, courtesy of JGI. **Page 13:** photo © Michael Nichols, courtesy NGS Image Collection. **Pages 14–15:** photo © Michael Neugebauer. **Page 16:** photo courtesy JGI. **Page 17:** Left: photo by Joan Travis, courtesy JGI; Center: photo by Hugo van Lawick, courtesy JGI; Right: photo courtesy JGI. **Pages 18–19:** All photos courtesy of Vanne Goodall. **Page 21:** photo courtesy JGI. **Page 22:** photo by Stephen Patch, courtesy JGI. **Page 23:** photo by Hugo van Lawick, courtesy NGS Image Collection. **Page 25:** photo by Stephen Patch, courtesy JGI. **Pages 26–27:** photo © Andy Nelson. **Page 28:** photos © Andy Nelson; map courtesy NGS Image Collection. **Page 29:** photo by Hugo van Lawick, courtesy JGI. **Page 30:** photo by Hugo van Lawick, courtesy NGS Image Collection. **Page 31:** photo by Hugo van Lawick, courtesy NGS Image Collection. **Page 32:** photo courtesy JGI. **Page 34:** photo courtesy JGI. **Page 35:** photo © Michael Nichols. **Page 37:** photo © Michael Nichols. **Pages 38–39:** photo © Michael Neugebauer. **Page 41, top row, left:** photo by Hugo van Lawick, courtesy JGI; **center:** photo courtesy JGI; **right:** photo by Hugo van Lawick, courtesy JGI. **Page 41, center row, left:** photo courtesy JGI; **center:** photo © Kristin J. Mosher, courtesy the Wildlife Collection; **right:** photo © Michael Nichols. **Page 41, bottom row, left:** photo © Michael Nichols; **center:** photo by Stephen Patch, courtesy JGI; **right:** photo © Andy Nelson. **Page 42, left:** photo courtesy JGI; **center:** photo courtesy JGI; **right:** photo © Kristin J. Mosher, courtesy

the Wildlife Collection. **Page 43, left:** photo © Michael Gunther; **right:** photo by Hugo van Lawick, courtesy NGS Image Collection. **Page 44:** photograph © Michael Nichols. **Pages 46–47:** photo © Michael Nichols. **Page 48:** photo by Stephen Patch, courtesy JGI. **Page 49:** photo by Janette Wallis, Ph.D., courtesy JGI. **Page 50:** photo by Hugo van Lawick, courtesy NGS Image Collection. **Page 51:** photograph © Michael Nichols. **Page 52:** photograph by Stephen Patch, courtesy JGI. **Page 53:** photo by Stephen Patch, courtesy JGI. **Page 54:** all photos by Stephen Patch, courtesy JGI. **Page 55:** photo courtesy JGI. **Page 56:** photo by Hugo van Lawick, courtesy JGI. **Page 57:** photo © Michael Nichols. **Page 58:** photo by Stephen Patch, courtesy JGI. **Page 59:** photo by Stephen Patch, courtesy JGI. **Page 60:** photo courtesy JGI. **Page 61:** photo by Stephen Patch, courtesy JGI. **Page 63:** photo by Stephen Patch, courtesy JGI. **Page 64:** photo courtesy JGI. **Page 65, top left and right:** photos by Stephen Patch, courtesy JGI; **bottom:** photo © Michael Nichols. **Page 66, top left:** photo by Stephen Patch, courtesy JGI; **bottom right:** photo by Michael Nichols. **Page 67, top:** photo © Michael Nichols; **bottom:** photo by Hugo van Lawick, courtesy the Jane Goodall Institute. **Page 68:** photo © Michael Neugebauer. **Page 70:** photo © Michael Nichols, courtesy NGS Image Collection. **Page 71:** photo © Andy Nelson. **Page 72:** photo © Michael Nichols. **Page 73:** photo by William R. Wallauer, courtesy JGI. **Page 74:** photo by William R. Wallauer, courtesy the Jane Goodall Institute. **Page 75:** photo by Stephen Patch, courtesy JGI. **Page 76:** photo © Michael Nichols. **Page 77:** photo © Michael Nichols, courtesy NGS Image Collection. **Page 79:** photograph ©

Michael Nichols, courtesy NGS Image Collection. **Page 80:** photo © Michael Nichols, courtesy NGS Image Collection. **Page 82:** photo © Michael Nichols, courtesy NGS Image Collection. **Page 83:** photo © Michael Nichols. **Page 84–85:** photo © Andy Nelson. **Page 86:** photo © Andy Nelson. **Page 87:** photo © Michael Nichols. **Page 88:** photo courtesy JGI. **Page 89:** photo by William R. Wallauer, courtesy JGI. **Page 90:** photo © Jennifer Krogh. **Page 91:** photo © Jennifer Krogh. **Page 92:** photo © Jennifer Krogh. **Page 93:** photo © Jennifer Krogh. **Page 94–95:** all photos © Michael Nichols. **Pages 96–97:** photo © Michael Nichols. **Page 98:** photo © Michael Nichols. **Page 99:** photo © Andy Nelson. **Page 100:** photo © Andy Nelson. **Page 101:** photo © Michael Nichols, courtesy NGS Image Collection. **Page 102:** photo © Michael Nichols, courtesy NGS Image Collection. **Page 103:** photo by Michael Neugebauer, courtesy JGI. **Page 104:** photo © Michael Nichols. **Page 107:** photo © Andy Nelson. **Page 108:** photo © Michael Nichols, courtesy NGS Image Collection. **Page 109:** photo © Michael Nichols. **Page 111:** photo © Andy Nelson. **Page 112:** photo courtesy JGI. **Page 113:** photo © Andy Nelson. **Page 114:** photo © Andy Nelson. **Page 115:** photo © Andy Nelson. **Page 116:** photo © Andy Nelson. **Page 117:** all photos © Andy Nelson. **Page 118:** photo © Andy Nelson. **Page 119:** photo © Andy Nelson. **Page 120:** photo © Michael Neugebauer, courtesy JGI. **Page 121:** photo © Michael Nichols, courtesy NGS Image Collection. **Page 122:** all photos © Michael Nichols, courtesy NGS Image Collection. **Page 123:** photo © Michael Nichols, courtesy NGS Image Collection. **Page 124:** photo courtesy JGI.

BIBLIOGRAPHY

CHILDREN'S BOOKS

Goodall, Jane. 1972. *Grub the Bush Baby*. Boston: Houghton Mifflin.

_____. 1988 (1996). *My Life with the Chimpanzees*. New York: Simon and Schuster.

_____. 1989. *The Chimpanzee Family Book*. Ridgefield, CT: The Jane Goodall Institute.

_____. 1989. *The Chimpanzee Family*. Canada: Madison Marketing Ltd.

_____. 1989. *Jane Goodall's Animal World: Chimps*. New York: Macmillan.

_____. 1999. *Dr. White*. New York: North-South Books.

ADULT BOOKS

Goodall, Jane. 1967. *My Friends the Wild Chimpanzees*. Washington, DC: The National Geographic Society.

van Lawick-Goodall, Jane and Hugo. 1970. *Innocent Killers*. Great Britain: Collins Clear-Type Press.

Goodall, Jane. 1971. *In the Shadow of Man*. Boston: Houghton Mifflin.

_____. 1986. *The Chimpanzees of Gombe: Patterns of Behavior*. Cambridge, MA: Belknap Press of Harvard University Press.

_____. 1990. *Through a Window*. Boston: Houghton Mifflin.

_____, and Dale Peterson. 1993. *Visions of Caliban: on Chimpanzees and People*. New York: Houghton Mifflin.

_____. 1994. *With Love*. New York: North-South Books.

_____. 1999. *Reason for Hope: A Spiritual Journey*. New York: Time Warner Books.

_____, and Nichols, Michael. 1999. *Brutal Kinship*. New York: Aperture.

VIDEOS AND DOCUMENTARIES

1963   *Miss Goodall and the Wild Chimpanzees*, National Geographic Society.

1984   *Among the Wild Chimpanzees*, National Geographic Special.

1990   *Chimpanzee Alert,* for the Nature Watch series, Central Television.

1990   *Chimps, So Like Us*, an HBO film.

1990   *My Life with the Chimpanzees*, National Geographic Society.

1990   *The Life and Legend of Jane Goodall*, National Geographic Society.

1990   *The Gombe Chimpanzees*, Bavarian Television.

1995   *Fifi's Boys*, for the Natural World series for the BBC.

1997   *Chimpanzee Diary* for BBC2 Animal Zone.

1997   *People of the Forest: The Chimps of Gombe*. Discovery Channel Video.

1999   *Reason for Hope*. KTCA, PBS Special.

NATIONAL GEOGRAPHIC ARTICLES

1963   My life with the wild chimpanzees. *National Geographic* 124 (2): 272-308.

1965   New discoveries among Africa's chimpanzees. *National Geographic* 128 (6): 802-831.

1967   (with H. van Lawick). Tool-using bird, the Egyptian Vulture. *National Geographic* 133 (5): 631-651.

1979   Life and Death at Gombe. *National Geographic* 155 (5): 592-621.

INDEX